MAXIMUM DAMAGE

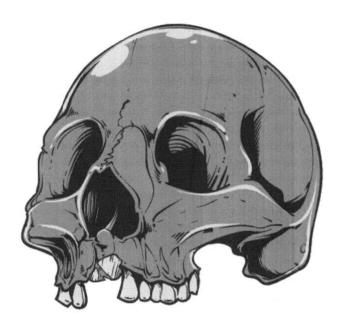

HIDDEN SECRETS BEHIND BRUTAL FIGHTING COMBINATIONS

Sammy Franco

D0939205

Maximum Damage

Also by Sammy Franco

First Strike: End a Fight in Ten Seconds or Less!
The Bigger They Are, The Harder They Fall
Self-Defense Tips and Tricks
Kubotan Power: Quick & Simple Steps to Mastering the Kubotan Keychain
The Complete Body Opponent Bag Book
Heavy Bag Training: Boxing, Mixed Martial Arts & Self-Defense
Gun Safety: For Home Defense and Concealed Carry
Out of the Cage: A Guide to Beating a Mixed Martial Artist on the Street
Warrior Wisdom: Inspiring Ideas from the World's Greatest Warriors
Judge, Jury and Executioner
Savage Street Fighting: Tactical Savagery as a Last Resort
Feral Fighting: Level 2 Widow Maker
The Widow Maker Program
War Craft: Street Fighting Tactics of the War Machine
War Machine: How to Transform Yourself Into a Vicious and Deadly Street
Fighter
1001 Street Fighting Secrets
When Seconds Count: Self-Defense for the Real World
Killer Instinct: Unarmed Combat for Street Survival
Street Lethal: Unarmed Urban Combat

Maximum Damage: Hidden Secrets Behind Brutal Fighting Combinations
Copyright © 2014 by Sammy Franco
ISBN: 978-1-941845-01-1
Printed in the United States of America

Published by Contemporary Fighting Arts, LLC.
P.O. Box 84028
Gaithersburg, Maryland 20883 USA
Phone: (301) 279-2244
Visit us Online at: www.SammyFranco.com

II

Contents

"Forewarned is forearmed."

- *English proverb*

Warning!

The information and techniques in this book can be dangerous and could lead to serious injury. The author, publisher, and distributors of this book disclaim any liability from loss, injury, or damage, personal or otherwise, resulting from the information and procedures in this book. This book is for academic study only.

Preface

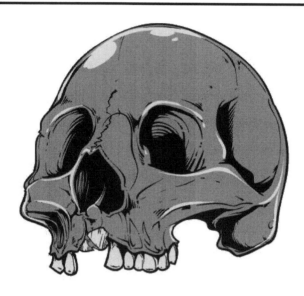

Maximum Damage teaches you the quickest ways to beat your opponent in the street by exploiting his physical and psychological reactions in a fight. Essentially, you will learn how to stay two steps ahead of your adversary by knowing exactly how he will react to your strikes before they are delivered.

In this book, I will teach you my Probable Reaction Dynamic method of fighting. Probable reaction dynamics (PRD) are both a scientific and comprehensive offensive strategy based on the positional theory of combat. Regardless of your style of fighting, PRD training will help you overpower your opponent by seamlessly integrating your strikes into brutal fighting combinations that are fast, ferocious and final!

Be careful, the information and techniques presented in this book are dangerous and should only be used to protect yourself or a loved one from the immediate risk of unlawful attack. Remember, the decision to use self-defense techniques must always be a last resort after all other means of avoiding violence have been exhausted.

Maximum Damage is both a skill-building workbook and strategic blueprint for combat. Feel free to write in the margins, underline passages, and dog-ear the pages. I strongly recommend that you read this text from beginning to end, chapter by chapter. Only after you have read the entire book should you treat it like a reference and skip around, reading those sections that interest you.

In addition, since many of the words in this book are defined within the context of Contemporary Fighting Arts and its related elements, I have provided a glossary.

I wish you all the best of luck in your training.

- Sammy Franco

Maximum Damage

VIII

Chapter One
Probable Reaction Dynamics Explained

"For every action, there is an equal and opposite reaction."

- Newton's Third Law

What Are Probable Reaction Dynamics?

Before we begin, it's imperative to first understand exactly what probable reaction dynamics (PRD) are, and how they directly relate to reality based self-defense. Essentially, probable reaction dynamics refer to your opponent's anticipated or predicted movements or actions during both armed and unarmed combat.

Probable reaction dynamics will always be the result or residual of your initial action. This action can be in the form of a verbal statement, physical technique, and even a simple gesture. The most basic example of probable reaction dynamics can be illustrated by the following scenario. Let's say, you are fighting with your adversary and the opportunity presents itself to forcefully kick him in his groin. When your foot comes in contact with its target, your opponent will exhibit one of several "possible" physical or psychological reactions to your strike. These responses might include:

- The opponent's head and body violently drop forward.

- The opponent grabs or covers his groin region.

- The opponent struggles for breath.

- The opponent momentarily freezes.

- The opponent goes into shock.

As I said earlier, probable reaction dynamics are not just limited to the physical plane of combat. As a matter fact, they can also result from verbal statements. For example, if you deliberately insulted a hot tempered or egotistical person, there's a good possibility he will become agitated or enraged with you. His emotional response to your action (in the form of words) is also a probable reaction dynamic.

When it comes to self-defense applications, probable reaction dynamics can be provoked one of three different ways:

- *Physically*
- *Verbally*
- *Gesticulatively*

For the purpose of this book, I'm only going to discuss *physical* probable reaction dynamics as they relate to striking combinations or compound attacks.

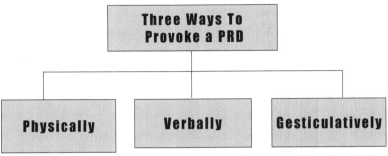

Probable reaction dynamics can be provoked three different ways: physically, verbally, and gesticulatively.

Physical Probable Reaction Dynamics

Physical probable reaction dynamics are the result of making physical contact with the adversary. Interestingly enough, this *"physical contact"* can either be unintentional or intentional.

Pictured here, a probable reaction dynamic to an eye strike.

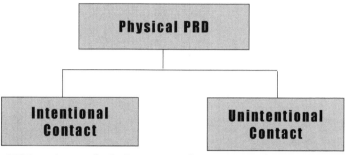

Physical PRD can be a result of either intentional or unintentional contact with your adversary.

Unintentional PRD

Here's an example of ***unintentional*** probable reaction dynamics. You are walking down the sidewalk and accidentally bump shoulders with a stranger. As you cross paths and make contact, the man stops, turns around and pushes you. In this situation, you do not have any idea what this man will do next. Much will depend on how well you diffuse the situation and the stranger's state of mind.

Intentional PRD

Intentional probable reaction dynamics, on the other hand, are a deliberate offensive strategy designed to maximize your chances of surviving a self-defense situation. With intentional PRD, you have a much better idea of the final outcome. Moreover, intentional probable reaction dynamics can be further classified into two categories: unarmed or armed combat.

Here's an example of *intentional* probable reaction dynamic. Let's use our previous scenario and take it one step further. After bumping shoulders with the man on the sidewalk, he pushes you and cocks his arm back to take a swing at your head. However, before he launches his punch, you immediately deliver a quick finger strike into his eyes.

The opponent's initial reaction (PRD) to your strike is to shut his eyes and temporarily freeze. For a nanosecond, his cognitive brain shuts down from the shock of your strike. At this very moment, you are given the opportunity to quickly escape from the altercation or follow-up with another debilitating strike.

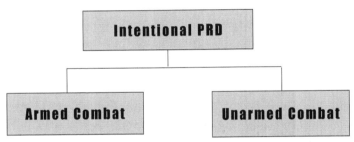

Intentional PRD can be used in both armed and unarmed combat situations.

Why PRD is Essential When Fighting

Knowledge of your assailant's probable reaction dynamics is vital in both armed and unarmed combat. In fact, you must be mindful of the possible reaction dynamics to every kick, punch, strike, and technique in your self-defense arsenal. This is exactly what I refer to as *"reaction dynamic awareness"* and I can assure you this is not such an easy task. However, by following the principles and concepts described in this book, it can be developed.

Regardless of your style of fighting (karate, muay thai, krav maga, boxing or mixed martial arts), understanding and ultimately mastering reaction dynamic awareness will give you a tremendous advantage when fighting. What follows is a list of these advantages:

PRD ADVANTAGES

- **Provides fighting foresight**
- **Compound attack efficiency**
- **Maintains the offensive flow**
- **Fight ends faster**
- **Conserves energy and reduces combat fatigue**
- **Reduces fear and apprehension**
- **Improves defensive awareness**
- **Anatomical target awareness**
- **Use-of-force accuracy**
- **Training time saver**

Fighting Foresight

Probable reaction dynamics gives you fighting foresight. Like a fortune teller, PRD enables you to predict or estimate (with reasonable accuracy) your opponent's action or reaction before your strike makes contact with his target. The ability to predict or forecast your opponent's target openings (which often translates to distance, angle, and vantage) in a fight is invaluable, especially if you're going to overwhelm him with a vicious compound attack.

Compound Attack Efficiency

Anyone who has experienced real fighting knows that in order to effectively neutralize a formidable opponent, you will almost always have to deliver more than a single punch or strike. Most unarmed combat situations will demand that you initiate a compound attack against your adversary. A compound attack is the logical sequence of two or more strikes thrown in strategic succession whereby you overwhelm the assailant's defenses with a flurry of full speed, full force blows.

Built on speed, power and target selection, the compound attack also requires calculation, control, and clarity. To maximize your offensive attack, you must have a thorough knowledge and understanding of the anatomical targets presented by your adversary. Unless your assailant is in full body armor, there are always targets. It simply is a matter of your recognizing them and striking quickly with the appropriate body weapons.

Your compound attack must also be efficient. Efficiency means that your strikes can reach their intended targets quickly and economically. Once again, possessing the foresight of knowing your opponent's next target opening will help you overwhelm him during a fight.

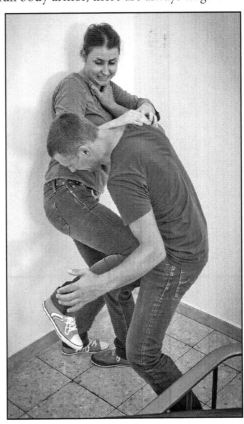

The ability to predict or foresee your opponent's physical reactions will give you a tremendous advantage in a self-defense situation. Pictured here, the probable reaction dynamics to a knee strike.

Maintains the Offensive Flow

The offensive flow is defined as a progression of continuous offensive movements designed to neutralize or (in some cases) terminate your adversary. When delivering a compound attack, it's vital that you maintain the pressure and don't stop until he is completely neutralized. Remember, stagnating your offensive flow (even for a second) can open you up to numerous dangers and risks in a fight.

Once again, by knowing beforehand where the opponent's next target will be, you'll be able to maintain the offensive flow and keep the pressure on the opponent.

Fights End Faster!

Every physical confrontation must end quickly. Remember, the longer a fight lasts, the greater your chances of serious injury or possible death. For those of you who are not convinced, here's a brief list of undesirable elements that can creep in as time passes during the course of a prolonged street fight.

- Spectators can intervene and possibly assist your opponent.

- Your assailant's friends can jump into the fight and assist him.

- You are at risk of

Prolonging a self-defense encounter is dangerous for both you and your loved ones.

making a tactical error that can cost you your life.

- Your immediate physical condition worsens which can lead to injury or death.

- Your friends or loved ones can get involved and possibly injured.

- The "adrenaline dump" will be completely depleted.

- The level of force between you and your adversary will progressively escalate.

Fortunately, reaction dynamic awareness enables you to quickly and efficiently neutralize your attacker in the shortest amount of time possible. Virtually no time is wasted and risks are minimized.

Conserves Energy and Reduces Combat Fatigue

If you are in above average shape, your ability to exert 100% effort in a fight will last approximately sixty seconds. Even with a

When fighting, it's essential to conserve as much energy as possible. This means all of your offensive techniques must be efficient.

maximum adrenaline dump, your energy level will drop significantly after one minute of all-out fighting.

Combat fatigue is a very real concern. It was the great American football coach Vince Lombardi who said, "Fatigue makes cowards of us all." Ironically, such words are applicable to reality based self-defense.

It's essential for you to conserve as much of your energy when fighting. Fortunately, mastering PRD awareness makes you an economical fighter, allowing you to conserve your energy during the severe stress of combat. In essence, every strike you launch will hit its intended target. There are no wasted punches and no unnecessary energy expenditure.

Reduces Fear and Apprehension

The more you know about fighting beforehand, the less you will fear during the actual encounter. PRD training provides direct insight to the real dynamics of unarmed combat. Once you become armed with this knowledge, you'll know exactly what to expect from your

The more you know about fighting beforehand, the less you will fear during the actual encounter.

opponent during a fight.

Moreover, PRD awareness provides a solid platform for combative preparedness. As I pointed out in my book, *The Bigger They Are, The Harder They Fall,* intimidation and fear are often caused by a lack of personal confidence. And confidence can only be acquired through proper training and strategic preparedness.

The good news is PRD training provides both cognitive and psycho motor preparedness by equipping you with the necessary information about the dynamics of combat.

Improves Defensive Awareness

Probable reaction dynamics are not only limited to offensive applications. As a matter of fact, PRD can also help you with defensive awareness. The fact is, the more you know about your opponent's PRD, the better prepared you will be if and when the tables are turned and you are faced with a defensive situation. The bottom line is, understanding the essence of probable reaction dynamics will help you better recover from an opponent's overwhelming attack.

Anatomical Target Awareness

Anyone who is seriously interested in incapacitating a formidable assailant must have a working knowledge and understanding of the body targets on the human anatomy. This is called target orientation.

Fortunately, target

orientation goes hand-in-hand with PRD awareness. Moreover, knowing how your opponent will react to a particular technique will help you better understand the medical implications of various self-defense strikes and techniques.

Use of Force Accuracy

As I have stated in some of my other books, every martial artist, self-defense student, combat specialist, and law enforcement officer has a moral and legal responsibility to know the medical implications of strikes and techniques. It is your responsibility to know which anatomical targets will stun, incapacitate, disfigure, cripple, or kill your assailant. PRD awareness helps reduce the risk of using excessive force in a fight. By knowing (beforehand) how your opponent will react to a strike, you'll be better able to curtail your compound attack to the bare minimum necessary to stop the threat.

Using excessive force in a fight can land you in jail. However, PRD awareness helps curtail your use of force response during a self-defense encounter.

Training Time Saver

Finally, PRD awareness will save you a lot of time when working out, especially for those of you who are specifically training for reality based self-defense encounters.

Unfortunately, for the vast majority of martial artists and self-defense practitioners, they will almost always combine fighting techniques in an arbitrary and somewhat whimsical fashion. Many practitioners have no strategic framework to follow and are often guided by *"how it feels."*

Consider the following example. During a typical heavy bag workout, a person will perform the following illogical combination (groin kick, jab, jab, hook punch, uppercut). While this is certainly a popular form of training, this particular heavy bag combination is not specifically tailored for the probable reaction dynamics of a real opponent in a fight. These offensive techniques simply don't relate to each other in a logical manner. In essence, the training is flawed from

If you are training for reality based self-defense, you must structure your fighting techniques in a logical manner.

the start.

Fortunately however, probable reaction dynamic awareness allows you to structure your combinations (that comprise a compound attack) in a logical manner geared specifically for real world combat encounters. By practicing the probable or likely striking combinations that occur in a real fight, you'll be better prepared if and when a real situation occurs.

PRD and Combination Fighting

Probable reaction dynamics should not be confused with traditional katas or forms. Essentially, katas are a series of prearranged movements based upon a response to imaginary attackers.

Unlike katas, PRD training does not require you to memorize a sequence of prearranged moves. Rather, the strategic objective behind PRD is to train your mind and body to efficiently transition from one "probable" offense technique to another. Remember, when using the PRD methodology, your offensive techniques will always be predicated on your opponent's movement.

By regularly practicing and developing your PRD combinations, you will refine and develop the necessary muscle memory to move quickly from one technique to the next with maximum efficiency and effectiveness.

PRD and Combat Sports

Probable reaction dynamic training is not just limited to reality-based self-defense applications. It can also be utilized in less precarious circumstances, such as sport combat training.

Mixed martial artists, boxers, kick boxers, and martial artists of all styles and backgrounds will also benefit greatly from understanding probable reaction dynamics. It can significantly

Probable reaction dynamics awareness can also benefit the mixed martial artist.

You can do a lot of damage in the boxing ring if you know how to exploit your opponent's probable reaction dynamics.

improve your fighting abilities in the ring.

Factors Influencing PRD

Most experienced and intelligent fighters will acknowledge that there are no absolutes in combat. As a matter of fact, your opponent's probable reaction dynamics are never guaranteed; they are simply possibilities or likely reactions that can occur.

Under most circumstances, you will be able to fully exploit your opponent's probable reaction dynamics to your advantage. However, there are certain factors and variables that can dramatically

Individuals who are emotionally disturbed or mentally ill are not immune to probable reaction dynamics.

alter or negate your opponent's PRD in a street fight. Some include: ineffectual technique, alcohol and psychoactive drugs.

Ineffectual Technique

You don't stand a chance of using PRD in a fight unless your offensive techniques are effective. This means the tools and techniques in your offensive arsenal must immediately produce the desired effect. Each and every strike must be fast, powerful, and accurate! Anything less can result in disaster.

Alcohol or Psychoactive Drugs

It's important to remember that alcohol and some psychoactive drugs like PCP can dull or negate some of the opponent's probable reaction dynamics. If your self-defense situation affords you the luxury of assessing your adversary prior to physical contact, try to determine his demeanor and general state of mind.

FACTORS INFLUENCING PRD

- **Ineffectual technique**
- **Alcohol**
- **Psychoactive Drugs**

Maximum Damage

Chapter Two
PRD Targets

"It is far more important to be able to hit the target than it is to haggle over who makes a weapon."

- Dwight D. Eisenhower

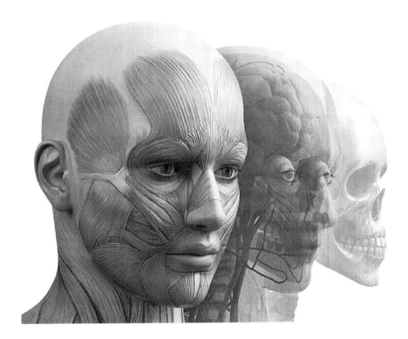

If you want to identify your opponent's probable reaction dynamics, you must also understand and master target orientation. Target orientation means having a workable knowledge of your opponent's anatomical targets. However, remember that knowledge and awareness is not enough, you must also possess the skills to strike these targets with extreme force and pinpoint accuracy.

When it comes to PRD applications, anatomical targets are split into one of two categories: primary and secondary.

Primary PRD Targets

Primary PRD targets are also known as *"first strike targets"* and they are one of several anatomical points that you must hit first in a fight. These primary targets generally pave the way for the opponent's initial probable reaction dynamics. However, primary targets can also be used as secondary targets in a fight. Primary PRD targets include: the eyes, nose, chin, temple, throat, groin, and thigh.

Secondary PRD Targets

Secondary PRD targets present themselves during the course of your compound attack. These targets include: the back of neck, ribs, solar plexus, knees, shins, fingers, instep, and toes.

The 3 Target Zones

For reasons of clarity, we can categorize both the primary and secondary anatomical targets into one of three possible zones.

Zone 1 (Head region) consists of targets related to your senses. This includes: the eyes, temples, nose, chin, and back of neck.

Zone 2 (Neck, Torso, Groin) consists of targets related to breathing. This includes: the throat, solar plexus, ribs, and testicles.

Zone 3 (Legs, Feet) consists of targets related to mobility. This includes: the thighs, knees, shins, instep, and toes.

PRD TARGET ZONES

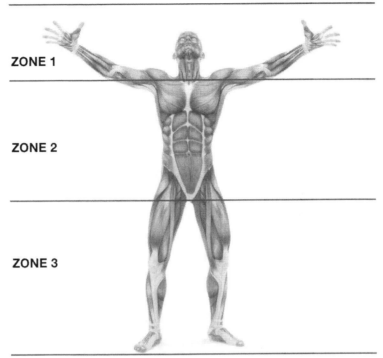

ZONE 1

ZONE 2

ZONE 3

Primary PRD Targets

Let's begin by discussing the primary PRD targets and the medical implications of each.

EYES

Eyes sit in the orbital bones of the skull. They are ideal targets for self-defense because they are extremely sensitive and difficult to protect, and striking them requires very little force. The eyes can be poked, scratched, and gouged from a variety of angles. Depending on the force of your

strike, it can cause numerous injuries, including watering of the eyes, hemorrhaging, blurred vision, temporary or permanent blindness, severe pain, rupture, shock, and unconsciousness.

Opponent's Probable Reaction Dynamic

The probable reaction dynamic from a well targeted eye strike may include the following:

- The opponent bends forward.

- The opponent shuts his eyes.

- The opponent covers his eyes with his hands.

- The opponent becomes temporarily immobilized.

- If temporary blindness occurs, the opponent might grab hold of you.

NOSE

The nose is made up of a thin bone, cartilage, numerous blood vessels, and many nerves. It is a particularly good target because it stands out from the criminal's face and can be struck from three different directions (up, straight, down). A moderate blow can cause stunning pain, eye-watering, temporary blindness, and hemorrhaging. A powerful strike can result in shock and unconsciousness.

Opponent's Probable Reaction Dynamic

The probable reaction dynamic from a strike to the nose may include the following:

- The opponent bends forward.

- The opponent shuts his eyes.

- The opponent covers his face with both his hands.

- The opponent becomes temporarily immobilized.

- If temporary blindness occurs, the opponent might grab hold of you.

CHIN

In boxing, the chin is considered a "knockout button," responsible for retiring hundreds of boxers. The chin is equally a good target for self-defense. When it is struck at a 45-degree angle, shock is transmitted to the cerebellum and cerebral hemispheres of the brain, 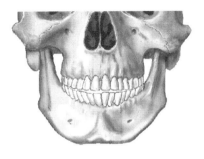 resulting in paralysis and immediate unconsciousness. Other possible injuries include broken jaw, concussion, and whiplash to the neck.

Opponent's Probable Reaction Dynamic

The probable reaction dynamic from a powerful chin strike may include the following:

- The opponent's head reels backward.

- The opponent's throat and torso become exposed.

- The opponent's centerline opens up.

- The opponent's arms and hands drop down.

- The opponent is knocked out cold.

TEMPLE

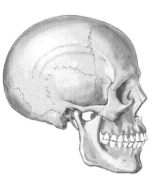

The temple or sphenoid bone is a thin, weak bone located on the side of the skull approximately 1 inch from the eyes. Because of its fragile structure and close proximity to the brain, a powerful strike to this target can be deadly. Other injuries include unconsciousness, hemorrhage, concussion, shock, and coma.

Opponent's Probable Reaction Dynamic

The probable reaction dynamic from a strike to the temple may include the following:

- The opponent's head and body fall sideways.
- The side of the opponent's torso become exposed.
- The opponent's eyes shut from the impact.
- The opponent's arms and hands drop down.
- The opponent is knocked out cold.

THROAT

The throat is a lethal target because it is only protected by a thin layer of skin. This region consists of the thyroid, hyaline and crocoid cartilage, trachea, and larynx. The trachea, or windpipe, is a cartilaginous tube that measures 4 1/2 inches in length and is approximately 1 inch in diameter. A powerful strike to this target can result in unconsciousness, blood drowning,

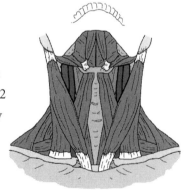

massive hemorrhaging, air starvation, and death. If the thyroid cartilage is crushed, hemorrhaging will occur, the windpipe will quickly swell shut, resulting in suffocation.

Opponent's Probable Reaction Dynamic

The probable reaction dynamic from a throat strike may include the following:

- The opponent's head and body drop forward.
- The opponent grabs or covers his throat with both hands.
- The opponent struggles for air.
- The opponent chokes and gags uncontrollably.
- The opponent goes into shock.

GROIN

Everyone man will agree that the genitals are highly sensitive organs. Even a light strike can be debilitating. A moderate strike to the groin can result in severe pain, nausea, vomiting, shortness of breath, and possible sterility. A powerful blow to the groin can crush the scrotum and testes against the pubic bones, causing shock and unconsciousness.

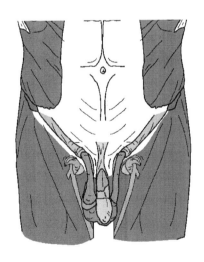

Opponent's Probable Reaction Dynamic

The probable reaction dynamic from a strike to the groin may include the following:

- The opponent's head and body violently drop forward.

- The opponent grabs or covers his groin region.

- The opponent struggles for breath.

- The opponent momentarily freezes.

THIGHS

Many people don't realize that the thighs are also vulnerable targets. A moderate kick to the rectus femoris or vastus lateralis muscles will result in immediate immobility of the leg. An extremely hard kick to the thigh can result in a fracture of the femur, resulting in internal bleeding, severe pain, cramping, and immobility of the broken leg.

Opponent's Probable Reaction Dynamic

The probable reaction dynamic from a strike to the thigh may include the following:

- The opponent looks down to the ground.

- The opponent's afflicted leg locks in place.

- The opponent's body weight shifts backwards.

- The opponent's body drops forward.

- The opponent's arms and hands come down to his sides.

- The opponent's centerline becomes vulnerable and exposed.

BACK OF NECK

The back of the neck consists of the first seven vertebrae of the spinal column. They act as a circuit board for nerve impulses from the brain to the body. The back of the neck is a lethal target because the vertebrae are poorly protected. A very powerful strike to the back of the neck can cause shock,

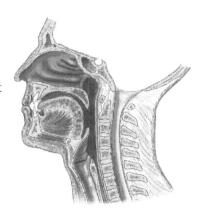

unconsciousness, a broken neck, complete paralysis, coma, and death.

Opponent's Probable Reaction Dynamic

The probable reaction dynamic from a strike to the back of neck may include the following:

- The opponent drops flat on the floor.

- The opponent is knocked out unconscious.

- The opponent falls forward and into your lower body.

RIBS

There are 12 pair of ribs in the human body. Excluding the eleventh and twelfth ribs, they are long and slender bones that are joined by the vertebral column in the back and the sternum and costal cartilage in the front.

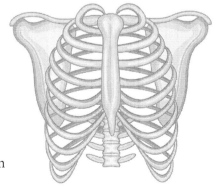

Since there are no eleventh and twelfth ribs (floating ribs) in the front, you should direct your strikes to the ninth and tenth ribs. A moderate strike to the anterior region of the ribs will cause severe pain and shortness of breath. A powerful 45-degree blow could easily break a rib and force it into a lung, resulting in its collapse, internal hemorrhaging, severe pain, air starvation, unconsciousness, and possible death.

Opponent's Probable Reaction Dynamic

The probable reaction dynamic from a strike to the ribs may include the following:

- The opponent's grabs and covers the afflicted rib with either one or both of his hands.

- The opponent doubles over in pain.

- The opponent's body bends forward.

- The opponent drops down on one knee.

- The opponent struggles for air.

SOLAR PLEXUS

The solar plexus is a large collection of nerves situated below the sternum in the upper abdomen. A moderate blow to this area will cause nausea, tremendous pain, and shock, making it difficult for the assailant to breathe. A powerful strike to the solar plexus can result in severe abdominal pain and cramping, air starvation, and shock.

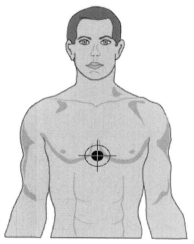

Opponent's Probable Reaction Dynamic

The probable reaction dynamic from a strike to the solar plexus may include the following:

- The opponent's grabs and covers the center of his chest with one or both of his hands.

- The opponent doubles over in pain.

- The opponent's body bends forward.

- The opponent drops down on one knee.

- The opponent struggles for air.

KNEES

The knee connects the femur to the tibia. It is a very weak joint held together by a number of supporting ligaments. When the assailant's leg is locked or fixed and a forceful strike is delivered to the front of the joint, the cruciate ligaments will tear, resulting in excruciating pain, swelling, and immobility.

Located on the front of the knee joint is the patella, which is made of a small, loose piece of bone. The patella is also extremely vulnerable to dislocation by a direct, forceful kick. Severe pain, swelling, and immobility will quickly result.

Opponent's Probable Reaction Dynamic

The probable reaction dynamic from a knee strike may include the following:

- The opponent looks down.
- The opponent's afflicted leg locks in place.
- The opponent's body weight shifts backwards.
- The opponent's body drops forward.
- The opponent's arms and hands drop down to his sides.
- The opponent's centerline becomes vulnerable and exposed.

SHINS

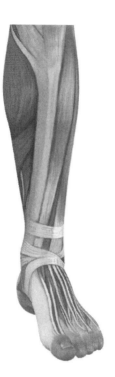

Everyone, at one time or another, has knocked his or her shin bone into the end of a table or bed accidentally and felt the intense pain associated with it. The shin is very sensitive because the bone is only protected by a thin layer of skin. However, a powerful kick delivered to this target can easily fracture it, resulting in nauseating pain, hemorrhaging, and immobility.

Opponent's Probable Reaction Dynamic

The probable reaction dynamic from a shin strike may include the following:

- The opponent looks down.
- The opponent's afflicted leg locks in place.
- The opponent's body weight shifts backwards.
- The opponent's body drops forward.
- The opponent's arms and hands drop down to his sides.

FINGERS

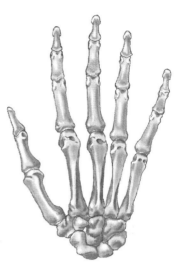

The fingers or digits are considered weak and vulnerable targets that can easily be jammed, sprained, broken, torn, and bitten. While a broken finger might not stop an attacker, it will certainly make him release his hold. A broken finger also makes it difficult for the assailant to clench his fist or hold a weapon. When attempting to break an assailant's finger, it's best to grab the pinkie and forcefully tear backward against the knuckle.

Opponent's Probable Reaction Dynamic

The probable reaction dynamic from an attack to the fingers may include the following:

- The opponent retracts his hand into his body.
- The opponent covers or protects his afflicted hand with his other hand.
- The opponent is incapable of clenching his fist or delivering a strike from the afflicted.
- The opponent is unable to maintain a grip on his weapon.
- If the opponent is holding or grabbing you, he will release his grip.

TOES/INSTEP

With a powerful stomp of your heel, you can break the small bones of an assailant's toes and or instep, causing severe pain and immobility. Stomping on the toes is an excellent technique for releasing many holds. It should be mentioned, however, that you should avoid an attack to the toes/instep if the attacker is wearing hard leather boots, i.e., combat, hiking, or motorcycle boots.

Opponent's Probable Reaction

Dynamic

The probable reaction dynamic from a strike to the toes or instep may include the following:

- The opponents will raise his afflicted leg off the ground.

- The opponent will look down to the ground.

- The opponent will experience difficulty walking.

PRD Target Exercises

Write down the different probable reaction dynamics to the following *primary* targets. Don't forget to include both offensive and defensive PRDs.

Groin

    1.

    2.

    3.

    4.

    5.

    6.

    7.

    8.

    9.

    10.

Thigh

    1.

    2.

    3.

    4.

    5.

    6.

    7.

    8.

    9.

    10.

Eyes

1.

2.

3.

4.

5.

6.

7.

8.

9.

10.

Nose

1.

2.

3.

4.

5.

6.

7.

8.

9.

10.

Throat

    1.

    2.

    3.

    4.

    5.

    6.

    7.

    8.

    9.

    10.

Temple

    1.

    2.

    3.

    4.

    5.

    6.

    7.

    8.

    9.

    10.

Chin

1.

2.

3.

4.

5.

6.

7.

8.

9.

10.

Now, Write down the different probable reaction dynamics to the following *secondary* PRD targets.

Back of Neck

1.

2.

3.

4.

5.

6.

7.

8.

9.

10.

Ribs

1.

2.

3.

4.

5.

6.

7.

8.

9.

10.

Solar Plexus

1.

2.

3.

4.

5.

6.

7.

8.

9.

10.

Knees

1.

2.

3.

4.

5.

6.

7.

8.

9.

10.

Shins

1.

2.

3.

4.

5.

6.

7.

8.

9.

10.

Fingers

1.

2.

3.

4.

5.

6.

7.

8.

9.

10.

Toes

1.

2.

3.

4.

5.

6.

7.

8.

9.

10.

Maximum Damage

Chapter Three
The Delivery System

"Approach combat in terms of black and white, but be prepared for gray."   **- Sammy Franco**

In order to make full use of your opponent's probable reaction dynamics, you'll need to master some important stances. When I say "stances" I am referring to a strategic posture you assume prior to and during unarmed combat. There are two:

- First Strike Stance
- Fighting Stance

Let's take a look at each one and see how they can be used to exploit your opponent's PRD.

The First Strike Stance and PRD

The first strike stance is used prior to delivering your preemptive strike and it sets the stage for setting up your opponent's probable reaction dynamics. The first strike stance facilitates "invisible deployment" of a preemptive strike while simultaneously protecting your vital targets against various possible counter attacks.

There are two variations of the first strike stance that needs to be mastered. They are:

- First Strike stance (for kicking & punching range)
- First Strike stance (for grappling range)

First Strike Stance (kicking & punching range)

This particular stance should be used when your adversary is standing in either kicking or punching range. To assume this stance, have both of your feet approximately shoulder width apart, knees slightly bent with your body weight evenly distributed over each leg. Blade your body at a 45-degree angle from your adversary. This position will help situate your centerline at a protective angle from your opponent, enhance your balance, promote mobility, and set up your first-strike weapons.

Next, make certain to hold your torso, pelvis, head, and back straight. And always stay relaxed and ready. Do not make the mistake of tensing your neck, shoulders, arms, or thighs. This muscular tension will most certainly throw off your timing, retard the speed of your movements, and telegraph your intentions.

Your hand positioning is another critical component of the first-strike stance. When confronted with an opponent in the kicking and punching ranges of unarmed combat, keep both of your hands open, relaxed, and up to protect the upper gates of your centerline. Both of your palms should be facing the opponent with your lead arm bent between 90 and 120 degrees, while your rear

The first strike stance for both kicking and punching ranges.

arm should be approximately eight inches from your chin.

Pictured here, the first strike stance in kicking range.

The first strike stance used in punching range of unarmed combat.

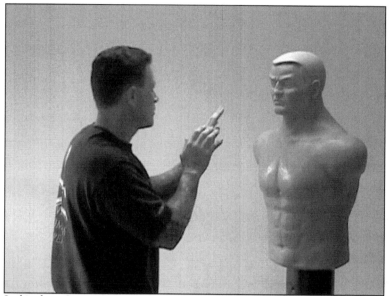

In this photo, Sammy Franco assumes a kicking/punching range first strike stance in front of the body opponent bag.

First Strike Stance (grappling range)

This variation of the first strike stance is used when you and your adversary are standing in grappling range. This stance is achieved by first blading your body at approximately 45- degrees from the adversary. Then keep both of your feet approximately shoulder-width apart, knees slightly bent,and your weight evenly distributed. *Important!* Place both of your hands side-by-side with your hands open, relaxed, and up to protect the upper gates of your centerline.

It's important to keep your torso, pelvis, head, and back erect. Stay relaxed and alert while remaining at ease. Once again, the key is avoiding any muscular tension - don't tighten up your shoulders, neck, arms or thighs.

The first strike stance for grappling range.

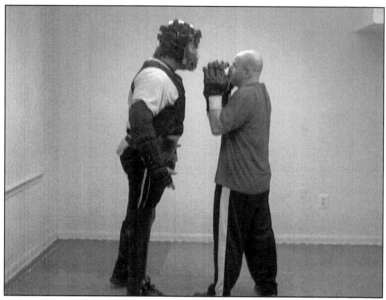

In this photo, the defender (right) assumes a first strike stance in the grappling range of unarmed combat.

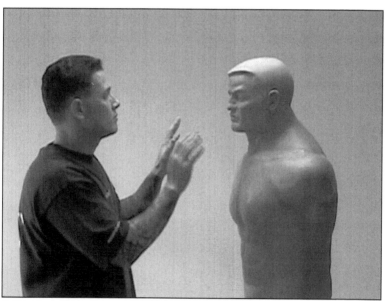

In this photo, the author assumes a grappling range first strike stance in front of the body opponent bag.

The Fighting Stance

The fighting stance is used when you're actually physically engaged with the opponent. This stance also functions as a *"reference point"* from where you will deliver your secondary strikes and exploit your opponent's reaction dynamics.

The fighting stance maximizes both offensive and defensive capabilities. It stresses strategic soundness and simplicity over complexity and style. The fighting stance facilitates optimum execution of your body weapons while simultaneously protecting your vital body targets against quick counter strikes. It is developed around the centerline.

The centerline is an imaginary vertical line passing through the center of the body, from the top of your head to the bottom of the groin. Most of your vital targets are situated along this line, including head, throat, solar plexus, and groin. Obviously, you want to avoid directly exposing your centerline to the assailant. To achieve this, position your feet and body at a 45-degree angle from the criminal. This moves your body targets back and away from direct attack but leaves you strategically positioned.

When assuming a fighting

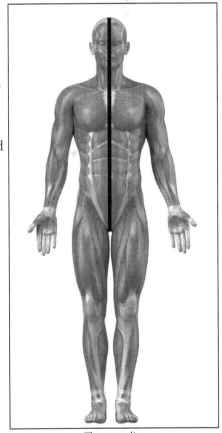

The centerline

stance, place your strongest, most coordinated side forward. For example, a right-handed person stands with his or her right side toward the assailant. Keeping your strongest side forward enhances the speed, power, and accuracy of your first strike. This doesn't mean that you should never practice fighting from your other side. You must be capable of fighting from both sides, and you should spend equal practice time on the left and right stances.

Many people make the costly mistake of stepping forward to assume a fighting stance. Do not do this! This action only moves you closer to your assailant before your protective structure is soundly established. Getting closer to your assailant also dramatically reduces your defensive reaction time. So get into the habit of stepping backward to assume your stance. Practice this daily until it becomes a natural and economical movement.

When assuming your fighting stance, place your feet about shoulder width apart. Keep your knees bent and flexible. Think of your legs as powerful springs to launch you through the ranges of unarmed self-defense (kicking, punching, grappling).

Mobility is also important, as we'll discuss later. All footwork and strategic movement should

Pictured here, the fighting stance.

be performed on the balls of your feet. Your weight distribution is another important factor. Since self-defense is dynamic, your weight distribution will change frequently. However, when stationary, keep 50 percent of your body weight on each leg and always be in control of it.

The hands are aligned one behind the other along your centerline. The lead arm is held high and bent at approximately 90 degrees. The rear arm is kept back by the chin. Arranged this way, the hands not only protect the upper centerline but also allow quick deployment of your body weapons. When holding your guard, do not tighten your shoulder or arm muscles prior to striking. Stay relaxed and loose. Finally, keep your chin slightly angled down. This diminishes target size and decreases the likelihood of a paralyzing blow to the chin or a lethal strike to the throat.

The best method for practicing your fighting stance is in front of a full-length mirror. Place the mirror in an area that allows ample room for movement; a garage or basement is perfect. Stand right in front of the mirror, far enough away to see your entire body. Stand naturally with your arms relaxed at your sides. Now shut your eyes and quickly assume your fighting stance. Open your eyes and check for flaws. Look for low hand guards, improper foot positioning or body angle, rigid shoulders and knees, etc.

Drill this way repeatedly, working from both the right and left side. Practice until your fighting stance becomes second nature.

Maximum Damage

Chapter Four
Hit Him First!

"When danger is imminent, strike first, strike fast, strike with authority, and keep the pressure on."   *-Sammy Franco*

What is a First Strike?

Whenever you are threatened by a dangerous adversary and it's impossible to escape safely, you must strike first, strike fast, strike with authority, and keep the pressure on. This offensive strategy is known as the first-strike principle, and it's essential to the process of neutralizing a formidable adversary in a self-defense altercation.

Basically, a first strike is defined as the strategic application of proactive force designed to interrupt the initial stages of an assault before it becomes a self-defense situation.

Pictured here, a short arc hammer fist strike delivered to the opponent's nose.

The Preemptive Strike and PRD

If your preemptive strike is delivered correctly, you are practically guaranteed a probable reaction dynamic from your opponent. As a matter of fact, it's your initial strike that determines your opponent's PRD. Essentially, your first strike technique "gets the ball rolling."

Therefore, it's very important to know the probable reaction dynamics to each and every first strike technique that you employ in a fight. Once you are made aware of the various probable reaction dynamics for each technique, you can then formulate logical secondary strikes that will comprise the rest of your compound attack.

Remember, PRD will always materialize from the preceding technique. For example, if your preemptive strike successfully creates a target opening, you would immediately follow up and attack with a secondary strike. If your secondary strike is effective, it would create another PRD. You would then exploit this target opening and so on and so on until your adversary no longer presents a threat to you.

First Strike Ranges

It's also important that you have a handful of first strike techniques that cover all three ranges of unarmed combat. These distances include the following:

- Kicking range
- Punching range
- Grappling range

The kicking range.

The punching range.

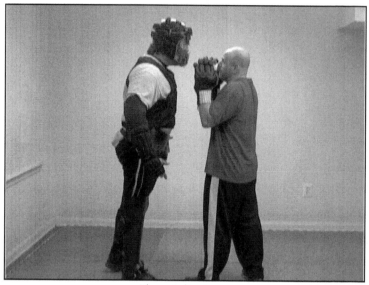

The grappling range.

First Strike Techniques

As I discussed in my book, *First Strike: End a Fight in Ten Seconds or Less*, there are numerous first strike techniques that you can employ in a self-defense situation. However, for the purposes of this book, I will only focus on five of them. They include:

- Vertical kick

- Push kick

- Finger Jab strike

- Rear Palm Heel strike

- Short Arc Hammer Fist

Vertical Kick

Push Kick

Finger Jab Strike

Rear Palm Heel Strike

Short Arc Hammer Fist

First Strike Review:

Vertical Kick

Push Kick

Finger Jab Strike

Rear Palm Heel

Short Arc Hammer Fist

Secondary Strike Techniques

Once your preemptive strike makes contact with its target, the opponent will present you with the first probable reaction dynamic. This is when secondary strike techniques will come into play. Secondary strikes are critical because they enable you to maintain the offensive flow and deliver a devastating compound attack.

While there are numerous secondary strike techniques, I'm only going to focus on the few of them. They include:

- Long arc hammer fist strike
- Vertical knee strike
- Uppercut punch
- Horizontal elbow strike
- Shovel hook punch
- Rear cross punch
- Rear hook punch
- Hook kick

Long Arc Hammer Fist Strike

Vertical Knee Strike

Uppercut Punch

Horizontal Elbow Strike

Shovel Hook Punch

Rear Cross Punch

Rear Hook Punch

Hook Kick

Secondary Strike Review:

Long Arc Hammer Fist Strike

Rear Vertical Knee

Uppercut Punch

Horizontal Elbow Strike

Shovel Hook Punch

Rear Cross Punch

Rear Hook Punch

Hook Kick

Maximum Damage

Chapter Five
PRD In Action

"The paradox of courage is that a man must be a little careless of his life even in order to keep it." - G. K. Chesterton

In this chapter, you're going to see probable reaction dynamics in action. Here, I've provided you with 20 PRD fighting scenarios illustrating both first and secondary strike techniques.

Remember that your opponent's probable reaction dynamics are alive and fluid. During the actual fight, you must be capable of adapting quickly to the ever changing situation. The ranges of unarmed combat and angles of attack will change rapidly so be on the lookout.

Finally, these scenarios serve only as examples of the possible combinations that you can deploy and a fight. We will start with the groin strike probable reaction dynamics.

Groin Strike PRD

The following sequence of photos will demonstrate some of the possible ways to exploit a kick to the opponent's groin.

The probable reaction dynamic from a strike to the groin might include the following:

- The opponent's head and body violently drop forward.

- The opponent grabs or covers his groin region.

- The opponent struggles to breath.

- The opponent momentarily freezes.

Possible Secondary Strikes based on PRD might include:

- Hammer first to back of neck

- Knee strike to face

- Uppercut punch to face

- Elbow strike to lateral side of face

- Hook punch to lateral side of face

Scenario #1: Vertical Kick PRD (Hammer fist)

Step 1: The defender (right) assumes a first strike stance.

Step 2: The defender attacks with a quick vertical kick to the groin.

Step 3: PRD response: The opponent reflexively drops his hands down.

Step 4: PRD response: The opponent leans forward and covers his groin.

Step 5: *The defender immediately follows up with a long arc hammer fist strike to the back of the opponent's neck.*

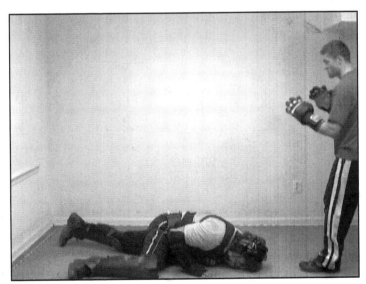

Step 6: *The opponent collapses to the floor.*

Scenario #2: Vertical Kick PRD (knee strike)

Step 1: The defender (right) is threatened at kicking range.

Step 2: He quickly launches a first strike.

Step 3: PRD response: The force of the kick elevates the opponent's body causing him to lose his balance.

Step 4: PRD response: The opponent's body drops forward into grappling range.

Step 5: The defender immediately counters with a vertical knee strike to the face.

Step 6: PRD response: The opponent falls to the floor.

Step 7: The defender disengages the range and assumes a protective stance.

Scenario #3: Vertical Kick PRD (uppercut punch)

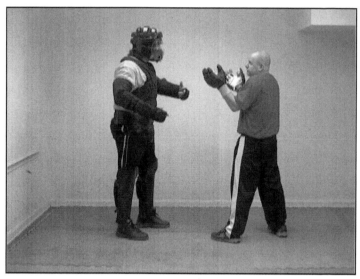

Step 1: The defender (right) attempt to de-escalate the situation.

Step 2: The defender is forced to deliver a vertical kick to the groin.

Step 3: PRD response: The opponent's body drops forward.

Step 4: PRD response: The opponent's head leans forward into punching range.

Step 5: The defender immediately follows up with an uppercut punch to the face.

Step 6: PRD response: The opponent loses his balance.

Step 7: PRD response: *The opponent's head and body fall backward.*

Step 8: *The defender disengages the range.*

Scenario #4: Vertical Kick PRD (horizontal elbow)

Step 1: The man on the left threatens the defender.

Step 2: The defender launches a preemptive strike.

Step 3: PRD response: The aggressor reflexively leans forward.

Step 4: The defender steps into grappling range.

Step 5: He immediately follows up with a horizontal elbow strike to the head.

Step 6: PRD response: The opponent's head and body are thrown sideways.

Step 7: PRD response: The opponent is stunned and disoriented.

Step 8: PRD response: The opponent falls to the ground.

Scenario #5: Vertical Kick PRD (combining secondary strikes)

Step 1: The defender assumes a first strike stance.

Step 2: He quickly launches a vertical kick to the groin.

Step 3: PRD response: The aggressor reflexively leans forward.

Step 4: The defender immediately follows up with a long arc hammer fist strike to the back of the opponents neck.

Step 5: PRD response: The opponent falls forward allowing the defender to deliver a vertical knee strike to the face.

Step 6: PRD response: The opponent falls to the ground.

Step 7: The defender relocates to a safe distance.

Scenario #6 Vertical Kick PRD (combining secondary strikes)

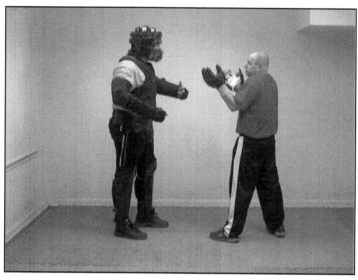

Step 1: The man on the right attempts to diffuse his hostile opponent.

Step 2: He delivers a vertical kick to the groin.

Step 3: PRD response: *The aggressor reflexively leans forward*

Step 4: *The defender steps into punching range.*

Step 5: He delivers an uppercut punch to the chin.

Step 6: Followed by a rear vertical knee.

Step 7: PRD response: The opponent falls to the ground.

Step 8: The defender retreats to the neutral zone.

Thigh Strike PRD

The following sequence of photos will demonstrate some of the possible ways to exploit a kick to the opponent's thigh. When striking the opponent's thigh, his probable reaction dynamic will include the following:

The probable reaction dynamic from a strike to the thigh may include the following:

- The opponent looks down to the ground.

- The opponent's afflicted leg locks in place.

- The opponent's body weight shifts backwards.

- The opponent's body drops forward.

- The opponent's arms and hands drop down to his sides.

- The opponent's centerline becomes vulnerable and exposed.

Possible Secondary Strikes based on PRD might include:

- Hammer first to back of neck

- Knee strike to face

- Uppercut punch to face

- Elbow strike to lateral side of face

- Hook punch to lateral side of face

Scenario #7: Push Kick PRD (Elbow strike)

Step 1: The man on the right assumes a first strike stance.

Step 2: He launches a push kick to his opponent's thigh.

Step 3: PRD response: The opponent's right leg locks into place and his weight shifts backwards.

Step 4: PRD response: The opponent's head leans forward.

Step 5: The defender launches a powerful horizontal elbow strike to the opponent's temple.

Step 6: PRD response: The opponent is knocked out cold.

Scenario #8 Push Kick PRD (uppercut punch)

Step 1: The defender assumes a first strike stance.

Step 2: He launches a first strike to his opponent's thigh.

Step 3: PRD response: The opponent's head and torso fall forward.

Step 4: The defender steps in with the rear uppercut punch.

Step 5: PRD response: The opponent falls backward.

Step 6: The defender quickly disengages from the opponent.

Scenario #9 Push Kick PRD (combining secondary strikes)

Step 1: The man on the right assumes a first strike stance.

Step 2: He launches a first strike to his opponent's thigh.

Step 3: PRD response: The opponent's head and torso fall forward.

Step 4: The defender steps in with the rear uppercut punch.

Step 5: PRD response: *The opponent grabs his head, reels backward, and exposes his centerline.*

Step 6: *The defender takes advantage by delivering a shovel hook to the opponent's ribs.*

Step 7: PRD response: The force of the blow forces the opponent sideways.

Step 8: PRD response: The opponent falls to the floor struggling for air.

Eye Strike PRD

The following sequence of photos will demonstrate some of the possible ways to exploit a strike to the opponent's eyes. When striking the opponent's thigh, his probable reaction dynamic will include the following:

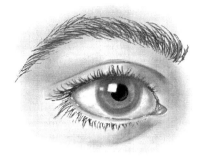

The probable reaction dynamic from a strike to the eyes may include the following:

- The opponent bends forward.

- The opponent shuts his eyes.

- The opponent covers his eyes with his hands.

- The opponent becomes temporarily immobilized.

- If temporary blindness occurs, the opponent might grab hold of you.

Possible Secondary Strikes based on PRD might include:

- Knee strike to groin

- Knee strike to face

- Uppercut punch to face

- Rear cross punch to the solar plexus

- Elbow strike to lateral side of face

- Hook punch to lateral side of face

Scenario #10 Finger Jab PRD (vertical knee)

Step 1: The defender (right) assumes a first strike stance in punching range.

Step 2: He delivers a finger jab strike to the opponent's eyes.

Step 3: PRD response: The opponent covers his eyes with both of his hands.

Step 4: The defender move in and engages the clinch.

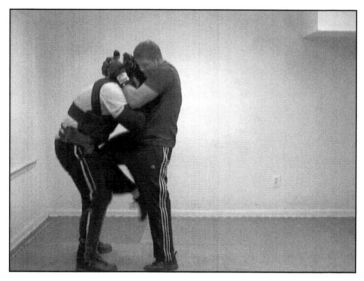

Step 5: He delivers a rear vertical knee strike to the opponent's groin.

Step 6: PRD response: The opponent loses his balance and stumbles.

Step 7: PRD response: The opponent falls to the floor.

Step 8: The defender disengages from the opponent.

Scenario #11 Finger Jab PRD (rear cross punch)

Step 1: The defender attempts to diffuse his hostile opponent.

Step 2: He quickly launches a swift finger jab strike to the eyes.

Step 3: PRD response: *The opponent covers both of his eyes and exposes his stomach to the defender.*

Step 4: *The defender delivers a powerful rear cross punch to the opponent's solar plexus.*

107

Step 5: PRD response: The opponent gets the wind knocked out him as he is driven backwards.

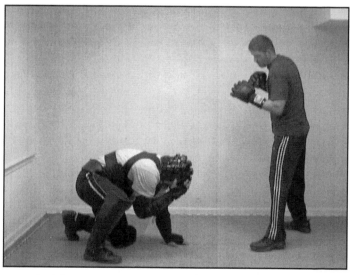

Step 6: The defender steps back and assesses the situation.

Scenario #12 Finger Jab PRD (rear hook punch)

Step 1: The man on the left threatens the defender.

Step 2: The defender launches a finger jab strike to the opponent's eyes.

Step 3: PRD response: The opponent covers his eyes with both of his hands.

Step 4: The defender delivers a hook punch to the side of the opponent's head.

Step 5: PRD response: The force of the blow knocks the opponent out.

Step 6: PRD response: The opponent falls to the floor.

Scenario #13 Finger Jab PRD (combining secondary strikes)

Step 1: The defender assumes a first strike stance.

Step 2: From a left lead stance, he launches a finger jab strike.

Step 3: PRD response: The opponent steps back and covers his eyes.

Step 4: The defender delivers a powerful rear cross punch to the opponent's solar plexus.

Step 5: The defender steps in and delivers a rear vertical knee strike to the opponent's groin.

Step 6: PRD response: The opponent drops to the floor.

Scenario #14 Finger Jab PRD (combining secondary strikes)

Step 1: The defender is threatened at the punching range of unarmed combat.

Step 2: From the first strike stance, he attacks with a quick finger jab strike to the eyes.

Step 3: The opponent is disoriented and covers both of his eyes with his hands.

Step 4: The defender delivers a powerful rear cross punch to the opponent's solar plexus.

Step 5: The defender immediately follows up with a powerful lead hook punch to the opponent's temple.

Step 6: PRD response: The opponent is knocked off balance and falls to the floor.

Nose Strike PRD

The following sequence of photos will demonstrate some of the possible ways to exploit a direct strike to the opponent's nose. When striking the opponent's nose, his probable reaction dynamic will include the following:

The probable reaction dynamic from a strike to the nose may include the following:

- The opponent bends forward.

- The opponent shuts his eyes.

- The opponent covers his face with both his hands.

- The opponent becomes temporarily immobilized.

- If temporary blindness occurs, the opponent might grab hold of you.

Possible Secondary Strikes based on PRD might include:

- Shovel hook to the opponent's ribs

- Hook kick to the opponent's thigh

- Rear cross to the opponent's solar plexus

- Elbow strike to the opponent's temple

- Knee strike to the opponent's groin

Scenario #15 Rear Palm Heel PRD (elbow strike)

Step 1: The defender is threatened at punching range.

Step 2: He launches a first strike to his opponent's nose.

Step 3: PRD response: The opponent covers his nose and leans backwards.

Step 4: PRD response: The opponent shuts his eyes and falls forward.

Step 5: The defender torques his body and strikes with a lead horizontal elbow.

Step 6: PRD response: The defender is knocked unconscious and falls to the ground.

Scenario #16 Rear Palm Heel PRD (rear knee strike)

Step 1: The defender assumes a first strike stance.

Step 2: He quickly launches a rear palm heel strike.

Step 3: PRD response: The opponent covers his face.

Step 4: The defender steps in and engages the clinch position.

Step 5: He immediately follows up with a vertical knee strike to the opponent's groin.

Step 6: PRD response: The opponent falls to the ground in agony.

Scenario #17 Rear Palm Heel PRD (shovel hook punch)

Step 1: The defender on the right assumes a first strike stands in punching range.

Step 2: He launches a rear palm heel strike to the opponent's nose.

Step 3: PRD response: The opponent reels back in pain exposing his torso to the defender.

Step 4: The defender takes advantage of his opponent's probable reaction dynamics and delivers a powerful shovel hook punch to his ribs.

Step 5: PRD response: The opponent's body flexes inward.

Step 6: PRD response: The opponent falls to the ground. The defender disengages the range.

Scenario #18 Rear Palm Heel PRD (hook kick)

Step 1: The man on the left threatens the defender.

Step 2: The defender quickly launches a rear palm heel strike to the opponent's nose.

Step 3: PRD response: The opponent is thrown backwards and knocked off balance.

Step 4: The defender takes advantage of his opponents position by delivering a devastating hook kick to his thigh.

Step 5: PRD response: The opponent is knocked off his feet.

Step 6: PRD response: The opponent drops to the floor.

Scenario #19 Short Arc Hammer Fist PRD (hook punch)

Step 1: The defender (right) attempts to de-escalate his threatening opponent.

Step 2: The attacker attempts to throw a punch.

Step 3: The defender beats him to the punch with a short arc hammer fist strike to the nose.

Step 4: PRD response: The opponent lowers his body and covers his face with both of his hands.

Step 5: The defender quickly recognizes the opening and launches a hook punch.

Step 6: PRD response: The opponents head and body are thrown to the side.

Scenario #20 Short Arc Hammer Fist PRD (knee strike)

Step 1: The defender is threatened at grappling range.

Step 2: He launches a short arc hammer fist strike to the bridge of the nose.

Step 3: PRD response: The opponent leans forward and covers his face with both of his hands.

Step 4: The defender steps in and engages the clinch position.

Step 5: The defender pulls the opponent's head downward and into a rear vertical knee strike.

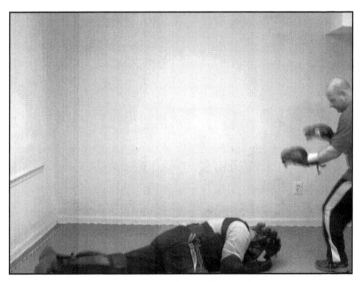

Step 6: PRD response: The opponent is knocked out cold.

Chapter Six
When Things Go Awry

" Self-preservation is the first principle of our nature."
- Alexander Hamilton

Offensive PRD

Probable reaction dynamics are not only limited to your opponent's defensive reactions. As a matter of fact, there might be times when your first strike doesn't provoke a defensive PRD from the adversary. Instead, he might respond with an attack of his own. This is known as *offensive* PRD. In such instances, you must prioritize defense and react to the opponent's counter assault.

There are several reasons why the opponent's PRD turns offensive or aggressive. They include the following:

- Your initial first strike lacks sufficient power.

- Your first strike misses the intended target.

- The opponent is high on drugs.

- Your secondary strike is telegraphic, slow or delayed.

- You or the opponent disengage from the range of engagement and it buys him a few seconds to gain his composure.

Regardless of its causes, offensive PRD is a valid concern. Therefore, I've included a few PRD scenarios illustrating how to deal with such a situation. Remember, in a street fight you must be prepared for anything and everything!

Scenario #1: Offensive PRD Example

Step 1: The defender on the right assumes a first strike stance.

Step 2: He quickly launches a short arc hammer fist strike to his opponent's nose.

Step 3: The hammer fist lacks sufficient power.

Step 4: The opponent quickly recovers from the hit.

Step 5: The opponent becomes enraged and prepares to counter attack.

Step 6: The opponent's offensive PRD is a hay maker to the head. The defender blocks the punch.

Step 7: The defender quickly engages the clinch position.

Step 8: And counters with a vertical knee strike to the opponent's groin.

Scenario #2: Offensive PRD Example

Step 1: The defender on the right assumes a first strike stance.

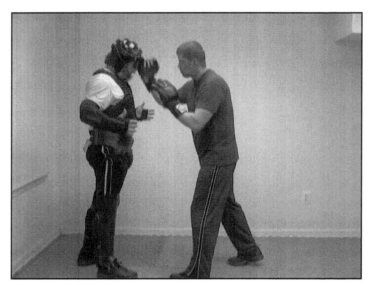

Step 2: He accidentally delivers a sloppy first strike.

Step 3: The strike misses the intended target.

Step 4: The opponent shakes it off.

Step 5: The man on the left charges in for a body tackle.

Step 6: The defender negates the upper body tackle with a stiff-arm jam technique.

Step 7: Once the opponent's forward energy is negated, the defender engages the clinch position.

Step 8: He quickly follows up with a rear vertical knee strike to the face.

Step 9: Defensive PRD response: The opponent covers his face and falls to the ground.

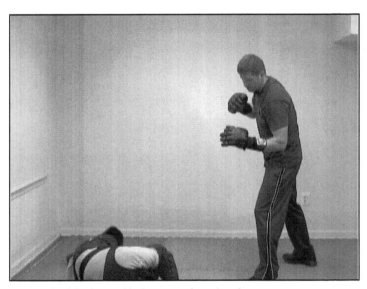

Step 10: The defender quickly disengages from the adversary.

Scenario #3: Offensive PRD

Step 1: The defender on the right assumes a first strike stance.

Step 2: His preemptive strike misses its target.

Step 3: The opponent becomes enraged.

Step 4: He swings at the defender's head.

Step 5: The defender blocks the punch.

Step 6: And quickly counters with a horizontal elbow strike to the opponent's head.

Step 7: Defensive PRD response: The defender is knocked unconscious and falls to the ground.

Chapter Seven
Getting the Most Out of PRD Training

" You never know what is enough unless you know what is more than enough." - **William Blake**

Now, it's time to look into probable reaction dynamic training. In this chapter, I'll show you some of the best ways to develop your PRD awareness skills. Let's begin with training equipment.

The Heavy Bag

While the heavy bag is great for developing striking power, it's not ideal for PRD training Some of you might be asking how this is possible. After all, the heavy bag is a tried-and-true piece of equipment used by every boxer, kick boxer, and mixed martial artists on the planet. While there's no disputing this fact, the heavy bag still falls short when it comes to PRD development.

True, the heavy bag is great for improving power, timing, and endurance, it however, is simply too large, heavy and slow to replicate realistic physiological reactions. This does not mean that you can't use the heavy bag for PRD training. You can! It's just that you must be exceptionally skilled at PRD awareness when using the bag.

The Body Opponent Bag

The body opponent bag (also called BOB) is a self-standing lifelike punching bag. The body opponent bag is superb for developing accurate striking techniques. Unfortunately, like the heavy

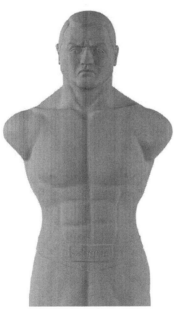

bag, the body opponent bag is a static target that doesn't react realistically when hit. Using the BOB for PRD training will require exceptional visualization skills and should only be reserved for the most advanced PRD practitioners.

The Double-End Bag

The double-end bag is a small leather ball suspended by a bungee cord. It is a valuable piece of training equipment that develops timing, accuracy, rhythm, coordination, footwork, and speed. This small bag also requires considerable practice and a lot of patience. In fact, it is perhaps one of the most difficult pieces of training equipment to master. Most beginners become very frustrated when working with the double-end bag because it can move erratically. To properly control the movement of the bag, you must hit it directly in the center. If you don't strike it dead center, it will bounce uncontrollably to the right and left.

Since the bag is very small and suspended by a bungee cord, your strikes are restricted to only one height level. This limitation renders it useless for PRD training.

Sparring

Full-contact sparring is certainly one of the best training exercises. It develops many combat attributes while conditioning your body for fighting. More importantly, sparring teaches you the importance of timing and judgment of distance in relation to your offensive and defensive techniques.

However, don't be misled. Never forget that sparring does not represent the violent dynamics and real danger of a vicious street fight. Sparring is nothing more than a training methodology used to develop specific combat attributes.

For most martial artists, full-contact sparring is a relatively safe activity. Sparring requires control and a mutual understanding of safety between you and your training partner. Generally, your goal is to *work with each other,* and not kill each other.

When it comes to PRD training, full-contact sparring has significant limitations.

Believe it or not, when it comes to PRD training, sparring has its limitations. Remember, in order to elicit a probable reaction dynamic from your opponent, he must feel intense pain. This means you would have to hit your training partner with a tremendous amount of force. Moreover, you would have to deliver this force to a vulnerable target such as the eyes, nose, chin, groin or throat. Otherwise, he won't react in a natural or realistic manner. Essentially, you would end up seriously injuring or crippling your training partner. So, this unfortunately eliminates sparring from effective PRD training.

Shadow Fighting

Shadow fighting is the creative deployment of offensive and defensive techniques and maneuvers against an imaginary opponent. It requires intense mental concentration, honest self-analysis, and a deep commitment to improve. If you are under a tight budget, the good news is that shadow fighting is inexpensive. All you need is a full-length mirror and a place to work out. The mirror is vital. It functions as a critic, your personal instructor. If you're truthful with yourself, the mirror will be too. It will point out every mistake - telegraphing, sloppy footwork, poor body mechanics, and even lack of physical conditioning.

Proper shadow fighting develops speed, power, balance, footwork, compound attack skills, sound form, and finesse. It even promotes a better understanding of combat ranges.

Like the heavy bag and body opponent bag, shadow fighting for PRD training requires exceptional visualization skills and a rock solid foundation in PRD awareness. Again, it should only be done by experienced PRD practitioners.

Focus Mitts and PRD Training

Let me be clear, focus mitts are the best tool for PRD training. As a matter of fact, if your training partner is well-versed at manipulating the mitts, you can realistically train your PRD skills.

While the focus mitts are exceptional for developing accuracy, speed, and timing in all offensive techniques, they are unmatched when it comes to PRD awareness and development. By placing the mitts at various angles and levels you can perform every conceivable kick, punch, or strike in your self-defense arsenal.

For those who don't know, the focus mitt is constructed of durable leather and is designed to withstand tremendous punishment. Your training partner (called the feeder) plays a vital role in focus mitt workouts by controlling the techniques you execute and the cadence of delivery.

When training with the mitts, try to work with an experienced feeder. The intensity and realism of your workout will depend largely upon the feeder's ability to effectively manipulate the mitts. A good focus mitt feeder knows how to safely push you to your physical limits. Most importantly, he must have a keen understanding and awareness of probable reaction dynamics.

The focus mitts will also allow you to practice your defensive skills against the opponent's offensive probable reaction dynamics. Unlike the heavy bag, body opponent bag and double and bag, your training partner can also attack you with the mitts. For example, your partner can swing at you from various angles to help refine blocking and parrying movements.

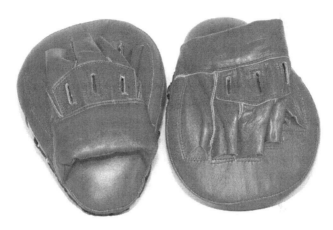

Pictured here, a pair of focus mitts.

A word of caution when using the focus mitts. Avoid the tendency to slam them into the oncoming blow. This will negate the effectiveness of your training partner's blow and possibly injure his wrist or hand.

Finally, when handling the focus mitts, you must provide a reasonable amount of resistance. This can be accomplished by tensing your hands and arms as the blow hits the surface of the mitt.

PRD Focus Mitt Combinations

To give you a head start in your training, I've included several focus mitt combinations demonstrating natural and realistic probable reaction dynamics.

Focus Mitt Drill #1 (Groin Kick PRD)

Step 1: The practitioner starts off with a first strike stance.

Step 2: Next, he begins with a vertical kick to the focus mitts.

Step 3: The feeder adjusts the focus mitts to simulate a realistic probable reaction dynamic target.

Step 4: The practitioner recognizes the PRD target and delivers a powerful hammer fist strike to the mitts.

Focus Mitt Drill #2 (Groin Kick PRD)

Step 1: The practitioner assumes a first strike stance.

Step 2: He begins with a vertical kick to the focus mitts.

Step 3: *The feeder moves forward to simulate a realistic probable reaction dynamic target.*

Step 4: *The practitioner recognizes the PRD target and moves in with a powerful vertical knee strike.*

Focus Mitt Drill #3 (Groin Kick PRD)

Step 1: The practitioner assumes a first strike stance.

Step 2: He launches a vertical kick to the focus mitts.

Step 3: The feeder adjusts the focus mitts to simulate a realistic probable reaction dynamic target.

Step 4: The practitioner recognizes the PRD target and delivers a powerful rear uppercut punch.

Focus Mitt Drill #4 (Push Kick PRD)

Step 1: The practitioner starts off with a first strike stance.

Step 2: He begins with a push kick.

Step 3: The feeder adjusts the focus mitts to simulate a realistic probable reaction dynamic target.

Step 4: The practitioner recognizes the PRD target and follows up with a rear uppercut punch.

Focus Mitt Drill #5 (Push Kick PRD)

Step 1: The practitioner assumes a first strike stance.

Step 2: He begins with a push kick.

Step 3: The feeder adjusts the focus mitts to simulate a realistic probable reaction dynamic target.

Step 4: The practitioner recognizes the PRD target and delivers a rear elbow strike.

Focus Mitt Drill #6 (Finger Jab PRD)

Step 1: The practitioner starts off with a first strike stance.

Step 2: Next, he delivers a finger jab strike.

Step 3: His training partner adjusts the focus mitts to simulate a realistic probable reaction dynamic target.

Step 4: The practitioner engages the clinch position and follows up with a rear vertical knee strike.

Focus Mitt Drill #7 (Finger Jab PRD)

Step 1: The practitioner assumes a first strike stance.

Step 2: Next, he delivers a finger jab strike.

Step 3: The feeder adjusts the focus mitts to simulate a realistic probable reaction dynamic target.

Step 4: The practitioner recognizes the PRD target and delivers a powerful rear cross punch to the mitts.

Focus Mitt Drill #8 (Finger Jab PRD)

Step 1: The practitioner starts off with a first strike stance.

Step 2: Next, he delivers a finger jab strike.

Step 3: His training partner adjusts the focus mitts to simulate a realistic probable reaction dynamic target.

Step 4: The practitioner delivers a powerful rear hook punch to the mitts.

Focus Mitt Drill #9 (Rear Palm Heel Strike PRD)

Step 1: The practitioner starts off with a first strike stance.

Step 2: Next, he delivers a rear palm heel strike.

Step 3: *The feeder adjusts the focus mitts to simulate a realistic probable reaction dynamic target.*

Step 4: *The practitioner recognizes the PRD target and attacks with a lead elbow strike.*

Focus Mitt Drill #10 (Short Arc Hammer Fist PRD)

Step 1: The practitioner starts off with a first strike stance in grappling range.

Step 2: He begins with a short arc hammer fist strike.

Step 3: The feeder adjusts the focus mitts to simulate a realistic probable reaction dynamic target.

Step 4: The practitioner recognizes the PRD target and delivers a powerful rear cross punch to the mitts.

Advanced PRD Focus Mitt Drills

The following photos illustrate an advanced form of PRD focus mitt training. This type of training differs from the previous examples for two reasons:

1. The practitioner (or striker) is unaware of which first strike he is required to deliver. This means the feeder must keep the focus mitts closed before he displays the first target. The instance the focus mitts are opened, the practitioner must immediately identify the first strike target and deliver the appropriate technique.

2. There is a greater emphasis on the "offensive flow." The striker is required to deliver a greater number of techniques in his compound attack. He must now identify multiple probable reactions targets during the drill.

Advanced PRD Combination #1

Step 1: The drill begins with the focus mitts closed. The practitioner on the right is unaware which first strike technique he will be required to deliver.

Step 2: The feeder immediately offers a first strike target.

Step 3: The striker recognizes the target (groin) and launches a vertical kick.

Step 4: The feeder adjusts the focus mitts to simulate a realistic probable reaction dynamic target.

Step 5: The practitioner recognizes the PRD target and delivers a powerful rear uppercut punch.

Step 6: The feeder maintains the position of the focus mitts indicating that another strike is required.

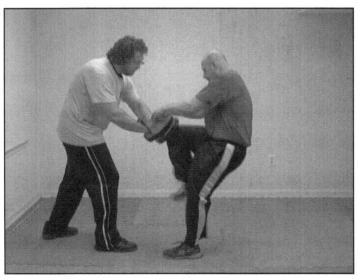

Step 7: The practitioner recognizes the next PRD target and moves in with a powerful vertical knee strike.

Advanced PRD Combination #2

Step 1: The drill begins with the focus mitts closed. The practitioner on the right is unaware which first strike technique he will be required to deliver.

Step 2: The feeder immediately offers a first strike target.

Step 3: The striker recognizes the target (eyes) and launches a finger jab.

Step 4: The feeder adjusts the focus mitts to simulate a realistic probable reaction dynamic target.

Step 5: The practitioner recognizes the PRD target and delivers a powerful rear cross punch.

Step 6: The feeder adjusts the focus mitts to simulate a new probable reaction dynamic target.

Step 7: The practitioner recognizes the new target and attacks with a lead elbow strike.

Step 8: Again, his training partner adjusts the focus mitts to simulate a third PRD target.

Step 9: The practitioner engages the clinch position and follows up with a rear vertical knee strike.

Think Outside the Box!

Focus mitt PRD training is not restricted to stand-up fighting. You can also develop striking techniques for the ground. What follows is a fundamental example of what you can do.

Step 1: The striker (top) prepares to launch his strike.

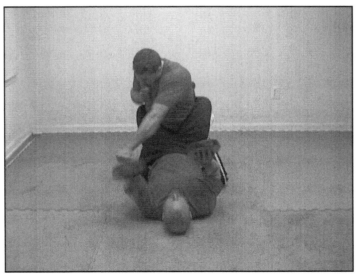

Step 2: Next, the feeder offers the first target.

Step 3: The feeder adjusts the focus mitts to simulate a new probable reaction dynamic target.

Step 4: The practitioner recognizes the new PRD target and delivers a diagonal elbow strike.

Step 5: The feeder switches to an offensive probable reaction. The defender parries the punch.

Step 6: The defender moves in with a biceps choke technique.

Step7: The PRD drill sequence is now complete.

Illogical Focus Mitt Combinations

The focus mitts offer tremendous freedom when training. As a matter of fact, you can perform just about any conceivable combination on the mitts. Frankly, you are only restricted by your own imagination.

Unfortunately, the freedom and flexibility of focus mitt training can sometimes present a serious problem for the PRD practitioner. It's very easy to make the mistake of piecing together illogical PRD combinations on the mitts. For example, while a PRD combination might feel fluid and natural on the mitts, it might fail miserably in a real encounter in the streets. Therefore, it's essential for you to analyze every PRD combination for its combat utility before imprinting it in your DNA.

The following photos will show you just how easy it is to fall into the trap of illogical focus mitt combinations.

Step 1: The practitioner on the right assumes a first strike stance.

Step 2: Next, he attacks with a push kick.

Step 3: The feeder raises the focus mitt giving the striker a new target.

Step 4: The striker throws a rear cross punch. At quick glance, this appears to be a natural and fluid compound attack, but in reality, it would never work in a real fight. The next sequence of photos will show you why.

Now, let's see the very same focus mitt combination applied in a real world combat situation.

Step 1: The defender (right) assumes a first strike stance.

Step 2: Next, he attacks with a push kick.

Step 3: PRD response: The opponent bends forward from the impact of the kick.

Step 4: The defender attempts a rear cross punch, but it's "choked." The opponent is simply too close for the punch to be effective.

Step 5: The opponent becomes enraged.

Step 6: He retaliates.

More PRD Resources

If you would like to learn more about probable reaction dynamics, be sure to see my Blitzkrieg in the Streets video, available on our website and Amazon.com.

Blitzkrieg in the Streets Instructional DVD

Blitzkrieg in the Streets Video Download

Glossary

The following terms are defined in the context of Contemporary Fighting Arts and its related concepts. In many instances, the definitions bear little resemblance to those found in a standard dictionary.

A

accuracy—The precise or exact projection of force. Accuracy is also defined as the ability to execute a combative movement with precision and exactness.

adaptability—The ability to physically and psychologically adjust to new or different conditions or circumstances of combat.

advanced first-strike tools—Offensive techniques that are specifically used when confronted with multiple opponents.

aerobic exercise—Literally, "with air." Exercise that elevates the heart rate to a training level for a prolonged period of time, usually 30 minutes.

affective preparedness – One of the three components of preparedness. Affective preparedness means being emotionally, philosophically, and spiritually prepared for the strains of combat. See cognitive preparedness and psychomotor preparedness.

aggression—Hostile and injurious behavior directed toward a person.

aggressive response—One of the three possible counters when assaulted by a grab, choke, or hold from a standing position. Aggressive response requires you to counter the enemy with destructive blows and strikes. See moderate response and passive response.

aggressive hand positioning—Placement of hands so as to imply aggressive or hostile intentions.

agility—An attribute of combat. One's ability to move his or her body quickly and gracefully.

amalgamation—A scientific process of uniting or merging.

ambidextrous—The ability to perform with equal facility on both the right and left sides of the body.

anabolic steroids – synthetic chemical compounds that resemble the male sex hormone testosterone. This performance-enhancing drug is known to increase lean muscle mass, strength, and endurance.

analysis and integration—One of the five elements of CFA's mental component. This is the painstaking process of breaking down various elements, concepts, sciences, and disciplines into their atomic parts, and then methodically and strategically analyzing, experimenting, and drastically modifying the information so that it fulfills three combative requirements: efficiency, effectiveness, and safety. Only then is it finally integrated into the CFA system.

anatomical striking targets—The various anatomical body targets that can be struck and which are especially vulnerable to potential harm. They include: the eyes, temple, nose, chin, back of neck, front of neck, solar plexus, ribs, groin, thighs, knees, shins, and instep.

assailant—A person who threatens or attacks another person.

assault—The threat or willful attempt to inflict injury upon the person of another.

assault and battery—The unlawful touching of another person without justification.

assessment—The process of rapidly gathering, analyzing, and accurately evaluating information in terms of threat and danger. You can assess people, places, actions, and objects.

attack—Offensive action designed to physically control, injure, or kill another person.

attitude—One of the three factors that determine who wins a street fight. Attitude means being emotionally, philosophically, and spiritually liberated from societal and religious mores. See skills and knowledge.

attributes of combat—The physical, mental, and spiritual qualities that enhance combat skills and tactics.

awareness—Perception or knowledge of people, places, actions, and objects. (In CFA, there are three categories of tactical awareness: criminal awareness, situational awareness, and self-awareness.)

B

balance—One's ability to maintain equilibrium while stationary or moving.

blading the body—Strategically positioning your body at a 45-degree angle.

blitz and disengage—A style of sparring whereby a fighter moves into a range of combat, unleashes a strategic compound attack, and then quickly disengages to a safe distance. Of all sparring methodologies, the blitz and disengage most closely resembles a real street fight.

block—A defensive tool designed to intercept the assailant's attack by placing a non-vital target between the assailant's strike and your vital body target.

body composition—The ratio of fat to lean body tissue.

body language—Nonverbal communication through posture, gestures, and facial expressions.

body mechanics—Technically precise body movement during the execution of a body weapon, defensive technique, or other fighting maneuver.

body tackle – A tackle that occurs when your opponent haphazardly rushes forward and plows his body into yours.

body weapon—Also known as a tool, one of the various body parts that can be used to strike or otherwise injure or kill a criminal assailant.

burn out—A negative emotional state acquired by physically over- training. Some symptoms include: illness, boredom, anxiety, disinterest in training, and general sluggishness.

C

cadence—Coordinating tempo and rhythm to establish a timing pattern of movement.

cardiorespiratory conditioning—The component of physical fitness that deals with the heart, lungs, and circulatory system.

centerline—An imaginary vertical line that divides your body in half and which contains many of your vital anatomical targets.

choke holds—Holds that impair the flow of blood or oxygen to the brain.

circular movements—Movements that follow the direction of a curve.

close-quarter combat—One of the three ranges of knife and bludgeon combat. At this distance, you can strike, slash, or stab your assailant with a variety of close-quarter techniques.

cognitive development—One of the five elements of CFA's mental component. The process of developing and enhancing your fighting skills through specific mental exercises and techniques. See analysis and integration, killer instinct, philosophy, and strategic/tactical development.

cognitive exercises—Various mental exercises used to enhance fighting skills and tactics.

cognitive preparedness – One of the three components of preparedness. Cognitive preparedness means being equipped with the strategic concepts, principles, and general knowledge of combat. See affective preparedness and psychomotor preparedness.

combat-oriented training—Training that is specifically related to the harsh realities of both armed and unarmed combat. See ritual-oriented training and sport-oriented training.

combative arts—The various arts of war. See martial arts.

combative attributes—See attributes of combat.

combative fitness—A state characterized by cardiorespiratory and muscular/skeletal conditioning, as well as proper body composition.

combative mentality—Also known as the killer instinct, this is a combative state of mind necessary for fighting. See killer instinct.

combat ranges—The various ranges of unarmed combat.

combative utility—The quality of condition of being combatively useful.

combination(s)—See compound attack.

common peroneal nerve—A pressure point area located approximately four to six inches above the knee on the midline of the outside of the thigh.

composure—A combative attribute. Composure is a quiet and focused mind-set that enables you to acquire your combative agenda.

compound attack—One of the five conventional methods of attack. Two or more body weapons launched in strategic succession whereby the fighter overwhelms his assailant with a flurry of full speed, full-force blows.

conditioning training—A CFA training methodology requiring the practitioner to deliver a variety of offensive and defensive combinations for a 4-minute period. See proficiency training and street training.

contact evasion—Physically moving or manipulating your body to avoid being tackled by the adversary.

Contemporary Fighting Arts—A modern martial art and self-defense system made up of three parts: physical, mental, and spiritual.

conventional ground-fighting tools—Specific ground-fighting techniques designed to control, restrain, and temporarily incapacitate your adversary. Some conventional ground fighting tactics include: submission holds, locks, certain choking techniques, and specific striking techniques.

coordination—A physical attribute characterized by the ability to perform a technique or movement with efficiency, balance, and accuracy.

counterattack—Offensive action made to counter an assailant's initial attack.

courage—A combative attribute. The state of mind and spirit that enables a fighter to face danger and vicissitudes with confidence, resolution, and bravery.

creatine monohydrate—A tasteless and odorless white powder that mimics some of the effects of anabolic steroids. Creatine is a safe body-building product that can benefit anyone who wants to increase their strength, endurance, and lean muscle mass.

criminal awareness—One of the three categories of CFA awareness. It involves a general understanding and knowledge of the nature and dynamics of a criminal's motivations, mentalities, methods, and capabilities to perpetrate violent crime. See situational awareness and self-awareness.

criminal justice—The study of criminal law and the procedures associated with its enforcement.

criminology—The scientific study of crime and criminals.

cross-stepping—The process of crossing one foot in front of or behind the other when moving.

crushing tactics—Nuclear grappling-range techniques designed to crush the assailant's anatomical targets.

D

deadly force—Weapons or techniques that may result in unconsciousness, permanent disfigurement, or death.

deception—A combative attribute. A stratagem whereby you delude your assailant.

decisiveness—A combative attribute. The ability to follow a tactical course of action that is unwavering and focused.

defense—The ability to strategically thwart an assailant's attack (armed or unarmed).

defensive flow—A progression of continuous defensive responses.

defensive mentality—A defensive mind-set.

defensive reaction time—The elapsed time between an assailant's physical attack and your defensive response to that attack. See offensive reaction time.

demeanor—A person's outward behavior. One of the essential factors to consider when assessing a threatening individual.

diet—A lifestyle of healthy eating.

disingenuous vocalization—The strategic and deceptive utilization of words to successfully launch a preemptive strike at your adversary.

distancing—The ability to quickly understand spatial relationships and how they relate to combat.

distractionary tactics—Various verbal and physical tactics designed to distract your adversary.

double-end bag—A small leather ball hung from the ceiling and anchored to the floor with bungee cord. It helps develop striking accuracy, speed, timing, eye-hand coordination, footwork and overall defensive skills.

double-leg takedown—A takedown that occurs when your opponent shoots for both of your legs to force you to the ground.

E

ectomorph—One of the three somatotypes. A body type characterized by a high degree of slenderness, angularity, and fragility. See endomorph and mesomorph.

effectiveness—One of the three criteria for a CFA body weapon, technique, tactic, or maneuver. It means the ability to produce a desired effect. See efficiency and safety.

efficiency—One of the three criteria for a CFA body weapon, technique, tactic, or maneuver. It means the ability to reach an objective quickly and economically. See effectiveness and safety.

emotionless—A combative attribute. Being temporarily devoid of human feeling.

endomorph—One of the three somatotypes. A body type characterized by a high degree of roundness, softness, and body fat. See ectomorph and mesomorph.

evasion—A defensive maneuver that allows you to strategically maneuver your body away from the assailant's strike.

evasive sidestepping—Evasive footwork where the practitioner moves to either the right or left side.

evasiveness—A combative attribute. The ability to avoid threat or danger.

excessive force—An amount of force that exceeds the need for a particular event and is unjustified in the eyes of the law.

experimentation—The painstaking process of testing a combative hypothesis or theory.

explosiveness—A combative attribute that is characterized by a sudden outburst of violent energy.

F

fear—A strong and unpleasant emotion caused by the anticipation or awareness of threat or danger. There are three stages of fear in order of intensity: fright, panic, and terror. See fright, panic, and terror.

feeder—A skilled technician who manipulates the focus mitts.

femoral nerve—A pressure point area located approximately 6 inches above the knee on the inside of the thigh.

fighting stance—Any one of the stances used in CFA's system. A strategic posture you can assume when face-to-face with an unarmed assailant(s). The fighting stance is generally used after you have launched your first-strike tool.

fight-or-flight syndrome—A response of the sympathetic nervous system to a fearful and threatening situation, during which it prepares your body to either fight or flee from the perceived danger.

finesse—A combative attribute. The ability to skillfully execute a movement or a series of movements with grace and refinement.

first strike—Proactive force used to interrupt the initial stages of an assault before it becomes a self-defense situation.

first-strike principle—A CFA principle that states that when physical danger is imminent and you have no other tactical option but to fight back, you should strike first, strike fast, and strike with authority and keep the pressure on.

first-strike stance—One of the stances used in CFA's system. A strategic posture used prior to initiating a first strike.

first-strike tools—Specific offensive tools designed to initiate a preemptive strike against your adversary.

fisted blows – Hand blows delivered with a clenched fist.

five tactical options – The five strategic responses you can make in a self-defense situation, listed in order of increasing level of resistance: comply, escape, de-escalate, assert, and fight back.

flexibility—The muscles' ability to move through maximum natural ranges. See muscular/skeletal conditioning.

focus mitts—Durable leather hand mitts used to develop and sharpen offensive and defensive skills.

footwork—Quick, economical steps performed on the balls of the feet while you are relaxed, alert, and balanced. Footwork is structured around four general movements: forward, backward, right, and left.

fractal tool—Offensive or defensive tools that can be used in more than one combat range.

fright—The first stage of fear; quick and sudden fear. See panic and terror.

G

grappling range—One of the three ranges of unarmed combat. Grappling range is the closest distance of unarmed combat from which you can employ a wide variety of close-quarter tools and techniques. The grappling range of unarmed combat is also divided into two planes: vertical (standing) and horizontal (ground fighting). See kicking range and punching range.

grappling-range tools—The various body tools and techniques that are employed in the grappling range of unarmed combat, including head butts; biting, tearing, clawing, crushing, and gouging tactics; foot stomps, horizontal, vertical, and diagonal elbow strikes, vertical and diagonal knee strikes, chokes, strangles, joint locks, and holds. See punching range tools and kicking range tools.

ground fighting—Also known as the horizontal grappling plane, this is fighting that takes place on the ground.

guard—Also known as the hand guard, this refers to a fighter's hand positioning.

guard position—Also known as leg guard or scissors hold, this is a ground-fighting position in which a fighter is on his back holding his opponent between his legs.

H

hand positioning—See guard.

hand wraps—Long strips of cotton that are wrapped around the hands and wrists for greater protection.

haymaker—A wild and telegraphed swing of the arms executed by an unskilled fighter.

head-hunter—A fighter who primarily attacks the head.

heavy bag—A large cylindrical bag used to develop kicking, punching, or striking power.

high-line kick—One of the two different classifications of a kick. A kick that is directed to targets above an assailant's waist level. See low-line kick.

hip fusing—A full-contact drill that teaches a fighter to "stand his ground" and overcome the fear of exchanging blows with a stronger opponent. This exercise is performed by connecting two fighters with a 3-foot chain, forcing them to fight in the punching range of unarmed combat.

histrionics—The field of theatrics or acting.

hook kick—A circular kick that can be delivered in both kicking and punching ranges.

hook punch—A circular punch that can be delivered in both the punching and grappling ranges.

I

impact power—Destructive force generated by mass and velocity.

impact training—A training exercise that develops pain tolerance.

incapacitate—To disable an assailant by rendering him unconscious or damaging his bones, joints, or organs.

initiative—Making the first offensive move in combat.

inside position—The area between the opponent's arms, where he has the greatest amount of control.

intent—One of the essential factors to consider when assessing a threatening individual. The assailant's purpose or motive. See demeanor, positioning, range, and weapon capability.

intuition—The innate ability to know or sense something without the use of rational thought.

J

joint lock—A grappling-range technique that immobilizes the

assailant's joint.

K

kick—A sudden, forceful strike with the foot.

kicking range—One of the three ranges of unarmed combat. Kicking range is the furthest distance of unarmed combat wherein you use your legs to strike an assailant. See grappling range and punching range.

kicking-range tools—The various body weapons employed in the kicking range of unarmed combat, including side kicks, push kicks, hook kicks, and vertical kicks.

killer instinct—A cold, primal mentality that surges to your consciousness and turns you into a vicious fighter.

kinesics—The study of nonlinguistic body movement communications. (For example, eye movement, shrugs, or facial gestures.)

kinesiology—The study of principles and mechanics of human movement.

kinesthetic perception—The ability to accurately feel your body during the execution of a particular movement.

knowledge—One of the three factors that determine who will win a street fight. Knowledge means knowing and understanding how to fight. See skills and attitude.

L

lead side -The side of the body that faces an assailant.

leg guard—See guard position.

linear movement—Movements that follow the path of a straight line.

low-maintenance tool—Offensive and defensive tools that require the least amount of training and practice to maintain proficiency. Low maintenance tools generally do not require preliminary stretching.

low-line kick—One of the two different classifications of a kick. A kick that is directed to targets below the assailant's waist level. (See high-line kick.)

lock—See joint lock.

M

maneuver—To manipulate into a strategically desired position.

MAP—An acronym that stands for moderate, aggressive, passive. MAP provides the practitioner with three possible responses to various grabs, chokes, and holds that occur from a standing position. See aggressive response, moderate response, and passive response.

martial arts—The "arts of war."

masking—The process of concealing your true feelings from your opponent by manipulating and managing your body language.

mechanics—(See body mechanics.)

mental attributes—The various cognitive qualities that enhance your fighting skills.

mental component—One of the three vital components of the CFA system. The mental component includes the cerebral aspects of fighting including the killer instinct, strategic and tactical development, analysis and integration, philosophy, and cognitive development. See physical component and spiritual component.

mesomorph—One of the three somatotypes. A body type classified by a high degree of muscularity and strength. The mesomorph possesses the ideal physique for unarmed combat. See ectomorph and endomorph.

mobility—A combative attribute. The ability to move your body quickly and freely while balanced. See footwork.

moderate response—One of the three possible counters when assaulted by a grab, choke, or hold from a standing position. Moderate response requires you to counter your opponent with a control and restraint (submission hold). See aggressive response and passive response.

modern martial art—A pragmatic combat art that has evolved to meet the demands and characteristics of the present time.

mounted position—A dominant ground-fighting position where a fighter straddles his opponent.

muscular endurance—The muscles' ability to perform the same motion or task repeatedly for a prolonged period of time.

muscular flexibility—The muscles' ability to move through maximum natural ranges.

muscular strength—The maximum force that can be exerted by a particular muscle or muscle group against resistance.

muscular/skeletal conditioning—An element of physical fitness that entails muscular strength, endurance, and flexibility.

N

naked choke—A throat choke executed from the chest to back position. This secure choke is executed with two hands and it can be performed while standing, kneeling, and ground fighting with the opponent.

neutralize—See incapacitate.

neutral zone—The distance outside the kicking range at which neither the practitioner nor the assailant can touch the other.

nonaggressive physiology—Strategic body language used prior to initiating a first strike.

nontelegraphic movement—Body mechanics or movements that do not inform an assailant of your intentions.

nuclear ground-fighting tools—Specific grappling range tools designed to inflict immediate and irreversible damage. Nuclear tools and tactics include biting tactics, tearing tactics, crushing tactics, continuous choking tactics, gouging techniques, raking tactics, and all striking techniques.

O

offense—The armed and unarmed means and methods of attacking a criminal assailant.

offensive flow—Continuous offensive movements (kicks, blows, and strikes) with unbroken continuity that ultimately neutralize or terminate the opponent. See compound attack.

offensive reaction time—The elapsed time between target selection and target impaction.

one-mindedness—A state of deep concentration wherein you are free from all distractions (internal and external).

ostrich defense—One of the biggest mistakes one can make when defending against an opponent. This is when the practitioner looks away from that which he fears (punches, kicks, and strikes). His mentality is, "If I can't see it, it can't hurt me."

P

pain tolerance—Your ability to physically and psychologically withstand pain.

panic—The second stage of fear; overpowering fear. See fright and terror.

parry—A defensive technique: a quick, forceful slap that redirects an assailant's linear attack. There are two types of parries: horizontal and vertical.

passive response—One of the three possible counters when assaulted by a grab, choke, or hold from a standing position. Passive response requires you to nullify the assault without injuring your adversary. See aggressive response and moderate response.

patience—A combative attribute. The ability to endure and tolerate difficulty.

perception—Interpretation of vital information acquired from your senses when faced with a potentially threatening situation.

philosophical resolution—The act of analyzing and answering various questions concerning the use of violence in defense of yourself and others.

philosophy—One of the five aspects of CFA's mental component. A deep state of introspection whereby you methodically resolve critical questions concerning the use of force in defense of yourself or others.

physical attributes—The numerous physical qualities that enhance your combative skills and abilities.

physical component—One of the three vital components of the CFA system. The physical component includes the physical aspects of fighting, such as physical fitness, weapon/technique mastery, and combative attributes. See mental component and spiritual component.

physical conditioning—See combative fitness.

physical fitness—See combative fitness.

positional asphyxia—The arrangement, placement, or positioning of your opponent's body in such a way as to interrupt your breathing and cause unconsciousness or possibly death.

positioning—The spatial relationship of the assailant to the assailed person in terms of target exposure, escape, angle of attack, and various other strategic considerations.

post-traumatic syndrome—A group of symptoms that may occur in the aftermath of a violent confrontation with a criminal assailant. Common symptoms of post-traumatic syndrome include denial, shock, fear, anger, severe depression, sleeping and eating disorders, societal withdrawal, and paranoia.

power—A physical attribute of armed and unarmed combat. The amount of force you can generate when striking an anatomical target.

power generators—Specific points on your body that generate impact power. There are three anatomical power generators: shoulders, hips, and feet.

precision—See accuracy.

preemptive strike—See first strike.

premise—An axiom, concept, rule, or any other valid reason to modify or go beyond that which has been established.

preparedness—A state of being ready for combat. There are three components of preparedness: affective preparedness, cognitive preparedness, and psychomotor preparedness.

probable reaction dynamics - The opponent's anticipated or predicted movements or actions during both armed and unarmed combat.

proficiency training—A CFA training methodology requiring the practitioner to execute a specific body weapon, technique, maneuver, or tactic over and over for a prescribed number of repetitions. See conditioning training and street training.

proxemics—The study of the nature and effect of man's personal space.

proximity—The ability to maintain a strategically safe distance from a threatening individual.

pseudospeciation—A combative attribute. The tendency to assign subhuman and inferior qualities to a threatening assailant.

psychological conditioning—The process of conditioning the mind for the horrors and rigors of real combat.

psychomotor preparedness—One of the three components of preparedness. Psychomotor preparedness means possessing all of the physical skills and attributes necessary to defeat a formidable adversary. See affective preparedness and cognitive preparedness.

punch—A quick, forceful strike of the fists.

punching range—One of the three ranges of unarmed combat. Punching range is the mid range of unarmed combat from which the fighter uses his hands to strike his assailant. See kicking range and grappling range.

punching-range tools—The various body weapons that are employed in the punching range of unarmed combat, including finger jabs, palm-heel strikes, rear cross, knife-hand strikes, horizontal and shovel hooks, uppercuts, and hammer-fist strikes. See grappling-range tools and kicking-range tools.

Q

qualities of combat—See attributes of combat.

R

range—The spatial relationship between a fighter and a

threatening assailant.

range deficiency—The inability to effectively fight and defend in all ranges of combat (armed and unarmed).

range manipulation—A combative attribute. The strategic manipulation of combat ranges.

range proficiency—A combative attribute. The ability to effectively fight and defend in all ranges of combat (armed and unarmed).

ranges of engagement—See combat ranges.

ranges of unarmed combat—The three distances (kicking range, punching range, and grappling range) a fighter might physically engage with an assailant while involved in unarmed combat.

reaction dynamics—see probable reaction dynamics.

reaction time—The elapsed time between a stimulus and the response to that particular stimulus. See offensive reaction time and defensive reaction time.

rear cross—A straight punch delivered from the rear hand that crosses from right to left (if in a left stance) or left to right (if in a right stance).

rear side—The side of the body furthest from the assailant. See lead side.

reasonable force—That degree of force which is not excessive for a particular event and which is appropriate in protecting yourself or others.

refinement—The strategic and methodical process of improving or perfecting.

relocation principle—Also known as relocating, this is a street-fighting tactic that requires you to immediately move to a new location (usually by flanking your adversary) after delivering a compound attack.

repetition—Performing a single movement, exercise, strike, or action continuously for a specific period.

research—A scientific investigation or inquiry.

rhythm—Movements characterized by the natural ebb and flow of related elements.

ritual-oriented training—Formalized training that is conducted without intrinsic purpose. See combat-oriented training and sport-oriented training.

S

safety—One of the three criteria for a CFA body weapon, technique, maneuver, or tactic. It means that the tool, technique, maneuver or tactic provides the least amount of danger and risk for the practitioner. See efficiency and effectiveness.

scissors hold—See guard position.

self-awareness—One of the three categories of CFA awareness. Knowing and understanding yourself. This includes aspects of yourself which may provoke criminal violence and which will promote a proper and strong reaction to an attack. See criminal awareness and situational awareness.

self-confidence—Having trust and faith in yourself.

self-enlightenment—The state of knowing your capabilities, limitations, character traits, feelings, general attributes, and motivations. See self-awareness.

set—A term used to describe a grouping of repetitions.

shadow fighting—A CFA training exercise used to develop and refine your tools, techniques, and attributes of armed and unarmed combat.

situational awareness—One of the three categories of CFA awareness. A state of being totally alert to your immediate surroundings, including people, places, objects, and actions. (See criminal awareness and self-awareness.)

skeletal alignment—The proper alignment or arrangement of your body. Skeletal alignment maximizes the structural integrity of striking tools.

skills—One of the three factors that determine who will win a street fight. Skills refers to psychomotor proficiency with the tools and techniques of combat. See Attitude and Knowledge.

slipping—A defensive maneuver that permits you to avoid an assailant's linear blow without stepping out of range. Slipping can be accomplished by quickly snapping the head and upper torso sideways (right or left) to avoid the blow.

snap back—A defensive maneuver that permits you to avoid an assailant's linear and circular blows without stepping out of range. The snap back can be accomplished by quickly snapping the head backward to avoid the assailant's blow.

somatotypes—A method of classifying human body types or builds into three different categories: endomorph, mesomorph, and ectomorph. See endomorph, mesomorph, and ectomorph.

sparring—A training exercise where two or more fighters fight each other while wearing protective equipment.

speed—A physical attribute of armed and unarmed combat. The rate or a measure of the rapid rate of motion.

spiritual component—One of the three vital components of the CFA system. The spiritual component includes the metaphysical issues and aspects of existence. See physical component and mental component.

sport-oriented training—Training that is geared for competition and governed by a set of rules. See combat-oriented training and ritual-oriented training.

sprawling—A grappling technique used to counter a double- or single-leg takedown.

square off—To be face-to-face with a hostile or threatening assailant who is about to attack you.

stance—One of the many strategic postures you assume prior to or during armed or unarmed combat.

stick fighting—Fighting that takes place with either one or two sticks.

strategic positioning—Tactically positioning yourself to either escape, move behind a barrier, or use a makeshift weapon.

strategic/tactical development—One of the five elements of CFA's mental component.

strategy—A carefully planned method of achieving your goal of engaging an assailant under advantageous conditions.

street fight—A spontaneous and violent confrontation between two or more individuals wherein no rules apply.

street fighter—An unorthodox combatant who has no formal training. His combative skills and tactics are usually developed in the street by the process of trial and error.

street training—A CFA training methodology requiring the practitioner to deliver explosive compound attacks for 10 to 20 seconds. See condition ng training and proficiency training.

strength training—The process of developing muscular strength through systematic application of progressive resistance.

striking art—A combat art that relies predominantly on striking techniques to neutralize or terminate a criminal attacker.

striking shield—A rectangular shield constructed of foam and vinyl used to develop power in your kicks, punches, and strikes.

striking tool—A natural body weapon that impacts with the assailant's anatomical target.

strong side—The strongest and most coordinated side of your body.

structure—A definite and organized pattern.

style—The distinct manner in which a fighter executes or performs his combat skills.

stylistic integration—The purposeful and scientific collection of tools and techniques from various disciplines, which are strategically integrated and dramatically altered to meet three essential criteria: efficiency, effectiveness, and combative safety.

submission holds—Also known as control and restraint techniques, many of these locks and holds create sufficient pain to cause the adversary to submit.

system—The unification of principles, philosophies, rules, strategies, methodologies, tools, and techniques of a particular method of combat.

T

tactic—The skill of using the available means to achieve an end.

target awareness—A combative attribute that encompasses five strategic principles: target orientation, target recognition, target selection, target impaction, and target exploitation.

target exploitation—A combative attribute. The strategic

maximization of your assailant's reaction dynamics during a fight. Target exploitation can be applied in both armed and unarmed encounters.

target impaction—The successful striking of the appropriate anatomical target.

target orientation—A combative attribute. Having a workable knowledge of the assailant's anatomical targets.

target recognition—The ability to immediately recognize appropriate anatomical targets during an emergency self-defense situation.

target selection—The process of mentally selecting the appropriate anatomical target for your self-defense situation. This is predicated on certain factors, including proper force response, assailant's positioning, and range.

target stare—A form of telegraphing in which you stare at the anatomical target you intend to strike.

target zones—The three areas in which an assailant's anatomical targets are located. (See zone one, zone two and zone three.)

technique—A systematic procedure by which a task is accomplished.

telegraphic cognizance—A combative attribute. The ability to recognize both verbal and non-verbal signs of aggression or assault.

telegraphing—Unintentionally making your intentions known to your adversary.

tempo—The speed or rate at which you speak.

terminate—To kill.

terror—The third stage of fear; defined as overpowering fear. See fright and panic.

timing—A physical and mental attribute of armed and unarmed combat. Your ability to execute a movement at the optimum moment.

tone—The overall quality or character of your voice.

tool—See body weapon.

traditional martial arts—Any martial art that fails to evolve and change to meet the demands and characteristics of its present environment.

traditional style/system—See traditional martial arts.

training drills—The various exercises and drills aimed at perfecting combat skills, attributes, and tactics.

U

unified mind—A mind free and clear of distractions and focused on the combative situation.

use of force response—A combative attribute. Selecting the appropriate level of force for a particular emergency self-defense situation.

V

viciousness—A combative attribute. The propensity to be extremely violent and destructive often characterized by intense savagery.

violence—The intentional utilization of physical force to coerce, injure, cripple, or kill.

visualization—Also known as mental visualization or mental imagery. The purposeful formation of mental images and scenarios in the mind's eye.

W

warm-up—A series of mild exercises, stretches, and movements designed to prepare you for more intense exercise.

weak side—The weaker and more uncoordinated side of your body.

weapon and technique mastery—A component of CFA's physical component. The kinesthetic and psychomotor development of a weapon or combative technique.

weapon capability—An assailant's ability to use and attack with a particular weapon.

Y

yell—A loud and aggressive scream or shout used for various strategic reasons.

Z

zone one—Anatomical targets related to your senses, including the eyes, temple, nose, chin, and back of neck.

zone three—Anatomical targets related to your mobility, including thighs, knees, shins, and instep.

zone two—Anatomical targets related to your breathing, including front of neck, solar plexus, ribs, and groin.

Maximum Damage

About The Author

With over 30 years of experience, Sammy Franco is one of the world's foremost authorities on armed and unarmed self-defense. Highly regarded as a leading innovator in combat sciences, Mr. Franco was one of the premier pioneers in the field of "reality-based" self-defense and martial arts instruction.

Sammy Franco is perhaps best known as the founder and creator of Contemporary Fighting Arts (CFA), a state-of-the-art offensive-based combat system that is specifically designed for real-world self-defense. CFA is a sophisticated and practical system of self-defense, designed specifically to provide efficient and effective methods to avoid, defuse, confront, and neutralize both armed and unarmed attackers.

CFA also draws from the concepts and principles of numerous sciences and disciplines, including police and military science, criminal justice, criminology, sociology, human psychology, philosophy, histrionics, kinesics, proxemics, kinesiology, emergency medicine, crisis management, and human anatomy.

Sammy Franco has frequently been featured in martial art magazines, newspapers, and appeared on numerous radio and television programs. Mr. Franco has also authored numerous books, magazine articles and editorials, and has developed a popular library of instructional videos.

Sammy Franco's experience and credibility in the combat science is unequaled. One of his many accomplishments in this field includes the fact that he has earned the ranking of a Law Enforcement Master Instructor, and has designed, implemented, and taught officer survival training to the United States Border Patrol (USBP). He instructs members of the US Secret Service, Military Special Forces, Washington DC Police Department, Montgomery County, Maryland Deputy Sheriffs, and the US Library of Congress Police. Sammy Franco is also a member of the prestigious International Law Enforcement Educators and Trainers Association (ILEETA) as well as the American Society of Law Enforcement Trainers (ASLET) and he is listed in the "Who's Who Director of Law Enforcement Instructors."

Sammy Franco is a nationally certified Law Enforcement Instructor in the following curricula: PR-24 Side-Handle Baton, Police Arrest and Control Procedures, Police Personal Weapons Tactics, Police Power Handcuffing Methods, Police Oleoresin Capsicum Aerosol Training (OCAT), Police Weapon Retention and Disarming Methods, Police Edged Weapon Countermeasures and "Use of Force" Assessment and Response Methods.

Mr. Franco is also a National Rifle Association (NRA) instructor who specializes in firearm safety, personal protection and advanced combat pistol shooting.

Mr. Franco holds a Bachelor of Arts degree in Criminal Justice from the University of Maryland. He is a regularly featured speaker at a number of professional conferences, and conducts dynamic and enlightening seminars on numerous aspects of self-defense and combat training.

For more information about Mr. Franco and his unique Contemporary Fighting Arts system, you can visit his website at: www.SammyFranco.com

If you liked this book, you will also want to read these:

FIRST STRIKE
End a Fight in Ten Seconds or Less!
by Sammy Franco

Learn how to stop any attack before it starts by mastering the art of the preemptive strike. First Strike gives you an easy-to-learn yet highly effective self-defense game plan for handling violent close-quarter combat encounters. First Strike will teach you instinctive, practical and realistic self-defense techniques that will drop any criminal attacker to the floor with one punishing blow. By reading this book and by practicing, you will learn the hard-hitting skills necessary to execute a punishing first strike and ultimately prevail in a self-defense situation. And that's what it is all about: winning in as little time as possible. 8.5 x 5.5, paperback, photos, illustrations, 202 pages.

OUT OF THE CAGE
A Complete Guide to Beating a Mixed Martial Artist on the Street
by Sammy Franco

Forget the UFC! The truth is, a street fight is the "ultimate no holds barred fight" often with deadly consequences, but you don't need to join a mixed martial arts school or become a cage fighter to defeat a mixed martial artist on the street. What you need are solid skills and combat proven techniques that can be applied under the stress of real world combat conditions. Out of the Cage takes you inside the mind of the MMA fighter and reveals all of his weaknesses, allowing you to quickly exploit them to your advantage. 10 x 7, paperback, photos, illustrations, 194 pages.

KUBOTAN POWER
Quick and Simple Steps to Mastering the Kubotan Keychain
by Sammy Franco

In this unique book, world-renowned self-defense expert, Sammy Franco takes thirty years of real-world teaching experience and gives you quick, easy and practical kubotan techniques that can be used by civilians, law enforcement personnel, or military professionals. Kubotan Power teaches you: tactical flashlight conversions, combat applications, grips, essential do's and don'ts, weapon nomenclature, impact shock, self-defense stages, high and low concealment positions, weapon deployment, target awareness, vital targets and medical implications, use of force considerations, attributes of fighting, defensive techniques, takedowns, training and flow drills, ground fighting, and much more. Whether you are a beginner or advanced, student or instructor, Kubotan Power shows you how to protect yourself and your loved ones against any thug you're likely to encounter on the street. 8.5 x 5.5, paperback, photos, illustrations, 204 pages.

Made in the USA
San Bernardino, CA
18 January 2015